A Fork in the Path to the Heavens

The Emergence of an Independent Space Force

Jeffrey R. Swegel

NIMBLE BOOKS LLC: THE AI LAB FOR BOOK-LOVERS
~ FRED ZIMMERMAN, EDITOR ~
Humans and AI making books richer, more diverse, and more surprising.

PUBLISHING INFORMATION

(c) 2024 Nimble Books LLC
ISBN: 978-1-60888-281-6

AI-GENERATED KEYWORD PHRASES

- Independent air forces emergence
- RAF in the United Kingdom
- Reasons for creation of separate air forces
- British and American experiences
- Debate over creation of separate Space Force
- United States
- Perspectives on creation of separate Space Force
- national defense
- Potential impact of separate Space Force on national defense
- United States' lead in aerospace dominance
- creating a separate Space Force.

PUBLISHER'S NOTES

Readers interested in space power should find this historic document valuable because it explores the emergence of independent air forces in the early 20th century, specifically focusing on the Royal Air Force in the United Kingdom and the United States Air Force. It examines the reasons behind the creation of separate air forces and compares the contemporary debate over the creation of a separate Space Force in the United States. This topic is relevant to current public issues surrounding the future of military capabilities in space and the potential need for a separate space-focused branch of the military. The document contributed to the dialogue a for United States Space Force.

This annotated edition illustrates the capabilities of the AI Lab for Book-Lovers to add context and ease-of-use to manuscripts. It includes several types of abstracts, building from simplest to more complex: TLDR (one word), ELI5, TLDR (vanilla), Scientific Style, and Action Items; essays to increase viewpoint diversity, such as Grounds for Dissent, Red Team Critique, and MAGA Perspective; and Notable Passages and Nutshell Summaries for each page.

ANNOTATIONS

Publishing Information iii
AI-generated Keyword Phrases iii
Publisher's Notes iii
Abstracts vi
    TL;DR (one word) vi
    Explain It To Me Like I'm Five Years Old vi
    TL;DR (vanilla) vi
    Scientific Style vi
    Action Items vii
Viewpoints viii
    Grounds for Dissent viii
    Red Team Critique ix
    MAGA Perspective xi
Page-by-Page Summaries xii
Notable Passages xviii

Abstracts

TL;DR (One Word)

Airpower.

Explain It To Me Like I'm Five Years Old

This document talks about how countries have created separate air forces, like the Royal Air Force in the UK. It explains why they did this and compares the UK and US experiences. It also talks about a current debate in the US about creating a separate Space Force. This would be a new military branch that focuses on space. The document talks about different opinions on this and how it could affect national defense. It ends by saying that the US should think about creating a Space Force to stay ahead in space.

TL;DR (Vanilla)

This document discusses the emergence of independent air forces, focusing on the RAF in the UK. It compares British and American experiences and examines the debate over a separate Space Force in the US. It suggests that the US should consider creating a Space Force to maintain dominance in aerospace.

Scientific Style

This document provides an analysis of the emergence of independent air forces, with a specific focus on the Royal Air Force (RAF) in the United Kingdom. It examines the motivations for establishing separate air forces and compares the experiences of both Britain and the United States. Furthermore, it explores the ongoing discussion surrounding the establishment of a separate Space Force in the United States, considering different viewpoints and potential implications for national defense. The document recommends that the United States should consider creating a separate Space Force to ensure its continued superiority in aerospace capabilities.

Action Items

Conduct further research on the history and development of independent air forces, including other countries' experiences.

Analyze the current debate over the creation of a separate Space Force in the United States, considering both sides of the argument.

Evaluate the potential impact of a separate Space Force on national defense and aerospace dominance.

Consider the necessary steps and resources required to establish a separate Space Force in the United States.

Assess the potential benefits and drawbacks of creating a separate Space Force for national security and technological advancement.

VIEWPOINTS

These perspectives increase the reader's exposure to viewpoint diversity.

GROUNDS FOR DISSENT

Cost: A member of the organization might dissent from this report due to the substantial cost associated with creating a separate Space Force. They may argue that allocating significant resources towards building an entirely new military branch would strain the overall defense budget, potentially leading to cuts in other critical areas such as ground troops or naval capabilities. This dissenting view might emphasize the need for fiscal prudence and prioritization of existing defense needs over the creation of a Space Force.

Duplication of Effort: Another principled reason for dissent could be the concern that a separate Space Force would duplicate efforts and capabilities already possessed by other branches of the military, particularly the Air Force. The dissenter might argue that space operations can effectively be integrated within existing structures, avoiding unnecessary bureaucracy and redundancy. They may believe that enhancing cooperation and coordination between different branches will yield more efficient and cost-effective outcomes compared to establishing a separate entity.

International Relations: A member of the organization might raise concerns about how the creation of a separate Space Force could impact international relations. They may argue that this move could be perceived as aggressive and militaristic by other nations, potentially escalating tensions in space-related activities. This dissenting view might advocate for maintaining a diplomatic approach to space affairs and prioritizing cooperative agreements with other countries rather than pursuing unilateral actions.

Strategic Focus: Some members may have principled reasons to dissent based on differing strategic priorities. They might argue that investing heavily in a separate Space Force detracts attention and resources from other pressing defense concerns such as cybersecurity, nuclear deterrence, or asymmetric warfare threats. This dissenting view might assert that focusing on conventional military capabilities and modernizing existing systems are more important for national security than developing a dedicated space-focused branch.

Organizational Challenges: A member might express principled dissent based on concerns about the practical challenges associated with establishing and managing a new military branch like a Space Force. They may highlight the difficulties of recruiting and retaining specialized personnel, developing a unique command structure, and fostering a distinct organizational culture. This dissenting view might emphasize the potential disruptions and inefficiencies that could arise during the transition period, impacting overall military effectiveness.

Ultimately, these principled dissenting views highlight potential drawbacks and concerns that justify a different perspective on the necessity and feasibility of creating a separate Space Force. They provide counterarguments to the conclusions reached in the document, contributing to a more robust discussion on this topic within the organization responsible for the report.

RED TEAM CRITIQUE

Overall, this document provides a comprehensive analysis of the emergence of independent air forces and examines the potential need for a separate Space Force in the United States. However, there are several areas where further elaboration and clarification would greatly enhance its effectiveness.

Firstly, while the document does discuss the reasons behind the creation of independent air forces, it could benefit from providing more specific historical examples to support its arguments. For instance, it briefly mentions the Royal Air Force in the UK but fails to delve into an in-depth analysis of their experience and any lessons that can be learned from it. By including case studies or specific incidents related to air force autonomy, the document would strengthen its credibility and provide readers with a clearer understanding of why independent air forces have emerged.

Similarly, when comparing British and American experiences with separate air forces, there is room for expansion. The document briefly acknowledges differences between these two nations but does not delve into these disparities or analyze their implications fully. By exploring contextual factors such as military structure, political climate, and defense priorities in both countries during their respective transitions toward independent air forces, readers would gain a deeper insight into what contributed to their varying paths.

Additionally, while discussing current debates over creating a separate Space Force within America's military establishment is pertinent to this topic; however, some vital perspectives may have been neglected. In particular, analyzing objections or critiques against establishing a distinct Space Force could offer greater nuance to this discussion. Considering viewpoints that argue for integrating space capabilities within existing branches rather than creating an entirely new service could provide additional depth and balance.

Moreover, the paper draws attention to potential impacts on national defense without fully examining alternative courses of action or counterarguments against establishing a separate Space Force. Providing well-researched rebuttals or alternative proposals within this domain could further enrich the debate around maintaining aerospace dominance.

Lastly, the conclusion advocating for creating a separate Space Force lacks sufficient support from evidence provided throughout most sections of this document. While the analysis of independent air forces is persuasive, it does not necessarily lead to an automatic endorsement for a separate Space Force. A more robust argument that builds off the historical context presented and effectively links it to the current situation would strengthen this conclusion.

In summary, while this document provides a substantial overview of the emergence of independent air forces and explores the potential need for a separate Space Force in the United States, further elaboration and consideration of counterarguments would greatly enhance its overall effectiveness. By incorporating historical case studies, analyzing objections against creating a distinct Space Force, and providing stronger support for its conclusion, this document could become an even more valuable resource for understanding these topics.

MAGA Perspective

This document is just another example of the liberal elite's obsession with creating separate entities to cater to their own agenda. The emergence of independent air forces, like the Royal Air Force in the UK, only serves to further fragment our military and weaken its overall strength. Instead of focusing on building a strong, unified defense force, they want to divert resources and attention towards creating separate branches. This is nothing more than a political move to pander to certain interest groups.

The comparison between the British and American experiences is irrelevant. The United States has always been the global leader in aerospace dominance, and we don't need to follow in the footsteps of other countries. Our military should remain united under one cohesive force, not divided into multiple branches that will only lead to bureaucratic inefficiencies and inter-service rivalries.

Furthermore, the discussion about a separate Space Force is nothing short of absurd. We already have organizations like NASA and the Air Force Space Command that handle our nation's space-related activities perfectly fine. Creating a separate entity would only duplicate efforts, waste taxpayer dollars, and feed into the left's desire for big government expansion.

The assertion that a separate Space Force would maintain our lead in aerospace dominance is laughable. Our dominance in aerospace is thanks to our innovation, technological superiority, and superior military capabilities - not because we have separate branches dedicated to specific domains. If anything, creating a separate Space Force would distract from these core strengths and undermine our national defense.

In conclusion, this document is yet another example of the liberal elite's attempt to push their own agenda onto our military. We should reject these efforts and instead focus on strengthening our existing forces rather than diluting them through unnecessary separation. MAGA stands for a strong, unified America - not a fragmented military serving special interests.

Page-by-Page Summaries

BODY-1   *The page discusses the emergence of an independent Space Force and its significance in military operations.*

BODY-2   *The monograph titled "A Fork in the Path to the Heavens, The Emergence of an Independent Space Force" by Maj Jeffrey R. Swegel has been approved by COL James K. Greer, Robert H. Berlin, and Philip J. Brookes from the School of Advanced Military Studies.*

BODY-3   *This page discusses the need for the United States to create an independent space force due to its technological advantages and the potential impact on national defense. It examines historical examples of creating independent air forces and evaluates current U.S. Army, Navy, and Air Force policies towards space capabilities. The author concludes that the current national space structure is hindering the development of U.S. space forces and recommends separating space forces similar to the creation of the USAF in 1947.*

BODY-4   *This page provides a table of contents for a document that compares and analyzes the emergence and development of the Royal Air Force, U.S. Air Force, and current concepts of space in terms of doctrine, training, leadership, organization, materiel, and soldiers.*

BODY-5   *The emergence of independent air forces in the 20th century required nations to develop new war-fighting mechanisms and doctrine. The reasons for the time disparity between the creation of separate air forces, such as the Royal Air Force and the U.S. Air Force, have not been fully explained.*

BODY-6   *The page discusses the ongoing debate within the USAF about the optimal mix of air and space forces. Some argue for renaming the Air Force to reflect its evolving capabilities, while others believe the current structure is sufficient. The Air Force currently has a significant number of personnel in its space command compared to the Army and Navy.*

BODY-7   *The monograph discusses the arguments for establishing a separate U.S. Space Force, including budget allocation, unique challenges in space, and potential adversaries closing the capabilities gap. It compares the decisions of Great Britain and the United States to establish separate air forces and uses the U.S. Army concept of Force Development as a framework to analyze various aspects.*

BODY-8   *This page discusses the processes of leader development, organizational development, materiel development, and soldier development in the Army. It also explores the comparison between current space capabilities and the concept of space operations in the U.S. Air Force to determine if a separate Space Force is necessary.*

BODY-9   *The Royal Air Force was established in 1912 as a separate military formation, but it did not fully address the issues facing British airpower. The German attacks in World War I challenged Britain's sense of security and traditional beliefs.*

BODY-10   *The page discusses the lack of strategic thinking in the British Army and Royal Navy regarding the use of aircraft during World War I, resulting in Germany's successful attacks on London. It also highlights the importance of offensive airpower over defensive measures.*

BODY-11   *The page discusses the challenges of air intercepts during World War I and the lack of coherent doctrine for the use of aircraft in the British Army. It highlights the need for a stronger offensive approach and a change in traditional ways of waging war.*

BODY-12 Trenchard believed that the airplane, specifically bombers, could quickly and effectively attack an enemy's manufacturing base to subdue them. He advocated for the formation of an independent air service due to the mismanagement of airpower by land and sea forces. Training of aviators during World War I was separate and based on each service's doctrine.

BODY-13 Formal schooling for aviators focused on technical aspects of aircraft, lacking instruction on military application. Lack of funding and neglect led to solving tactical problems in the field. Senior leaders hindered cooperation between air services due to parochial views and ingrained attitudes towards war.

BODY-14 During World War I, both the army and navy had a limited understanding of airpower and failed to organize their aircraft effectively. The lack of visionary leaders hindered the development and utilization of air power, particularly in the Royal Naval Air Service. Many naval airmen left for the Royal Air Force due to institutional constraints.

BODY-15 The page discusses the need for leader development in the air arm and the inter-service rivalry between the Royal Navy and British Army in terms of aviation assets and operations. This rivalry delayed implementation of recommendations and resulted in a lack of coherent national air policy.

BODY-16 The page discusses the parochial thinking and lack of unity in command within the British air organizations during World War I, highlighting the need for a more strategic and coordinated approach to airpower.

BODY-17 The page discusses the challenges of consolidating air power during World War I and the need for a centralized system to achieve efficiency and strategic effectiveness. It highlights the success of Hugh Trenchard in demonstrating the importance of massing air assets under a single command.

BODY-18 The page discusses the challenges faced by the British air arms during World War I, including technological advancements and recruitment difficulties. The development of British air power was driven by competition between the Navy and Army rather than operational necessity.

BODY-19 During World War I, there was a shortage of pilots and mechanics in the British military. The Army and Navy did not prioritize aviation and lacked proper training and support for their aviation personnel. This led to resistance from branches when individuals were transferred to the air force. The Royal Navy had little understanding or respect for aviation, causing many aviators to leave once the Royal Air Force was formed.

BODY-20 The page discusses the Navy's efforts to regain control over its tactical aviation, which were partially successful in the following decade.

BODY-21 The National Security Act of 1947 created the U.S. Air Force as part of the Department of Defense, fulfilling the vision of American airpower advocates. The conditions faced by the U.S. military were similar to those in Britain, and influential figures like Billy Mitchell played a role in advocating for an independent air service.

BODY-22 The page discusses the early perception of airpower in the United States, particularly in the Navy, during World War I. It highlights the debate between fixed wing aircraft and balloons, and how airpower was seen as a means to support naval battles.

BODY-23 The page discusses principles of employment for the air arm, including the importance of air superiority and offensive attacks against enemy air forces. It also mentions the need for concentrated command and the Army's acceptance of proper

	air application. The Navy made limited progress in using aviation for battlefield-wide effects.
BODY-24	*The page discusses the shift in naval thinking about aircraft carriers after World War I and the development of naval air theory and doctrine. The Navy saw aircraft as support for the fleet's great battle, with roles including reconnaissance and attacking enemy battleships.*
BODY-25	*The page discusses the lack of formal training and neglect of aviation in the US Army during World War I, resulting in a lack of suitable aircraft for advanced training.*
BODY-26	*The page discusses the American military's lack of coordination and integration of air power during World War I, leading to dependence on European training facilities. The need for a dedicated school for air education is highlighted, while the Navy continues to prioritize surface warfare over aviation.*
BODY-27	*Advocates for the separation of the Air Force from the Army faced opposition, but with key supporters and lessons learned from past wars, they achieved some success. Carl Spaatz and Billy Mitchell played important roles in the development of the air arm.*
BODY-28	*Many leaders in the War Department and government did not see the need for an independent air force due to the isolation of the US. The Navy also did not prioritize developing specialists in air power. The US Army Air Force organization started in 1907 and later Congress established it as a separate department.*
BODY-29	*During the inter-war years, the US Army Air Service relied on British strategies and prioritized direct support of ground troops over strategic airpower. The Navy also underwent a command structure change to increase cooperation and eliminate problems caused by a distinction between line officers and engineer officers.*
BODY-30	*The page discusses the U.S. Navy's resistance to developing a naval air corps and their use of individual aircraft attached to fleets during World War I. It also mentions issues with control designs and lack of funding for aviation prior to the war.*
BODY-31	*The post-war U.S. Air Corps struggled with disorganized procurement and inconsistent funding, resulting in a below-par aircraft industry and air force. This led to friction within the Army and challenges from Congress regarding their plans for air support.*
BODY-32	*During World War I, the US Army lacked trained airmen and did not prioritize aviation. This led to a shortage of officers and enlisted men with knowledge of air power. The Air Service Field Officer's School was established as a partial solution, but it did not fully address the problem. The Navy also failed to make significant changes in their education courses related to air power.*
BODY-33	*The development of airmen in the military was hindered by the services' reluctance to prioritize air power, but this changed during World War II when soldiers and sailors were directly inducted into air arms. However, the army initially made mistakes in not assigning air officers to teaching staffs.*
BODY-34	*The chapter discusses the creation of U.S. Space Command and the challenges in defining command roles in space operations. It highlights the increasing reliance on space capabilities and the resulting tension between services competing for resources. The Air Force's role as executive agent for space has also caused uneasiness among other branches.*

BODY-35   The Air Force incorporates space forces into its doctrine and recognizes the need to defend US space assets while denying adversaries' access to them.

BODY-36   The Army and Navy both incorporate space applications into their regular doctrine, with the Army emphasizing support for land forces and the Navy focusing on providing space-based support to warfighters. The Navy is beginning to develop publications on naval space operations but still has some weaknesses in its space program.

BODY-37   The page discusses the erosion of the effectiveness of the Department of Navy's space strategy, including diffused management responsibilities and lack of integrated management of human resources. It also mentions progress in integrating space capabilities into training exercises for the Air Force and Army.

BODY-38   The page discusses the need for space awareness training and education for individuals and units in the military, particularly in the Navy. It also mentions the lack of leadership from space specialists in commanding positions and the limited curriculum on space operations in military education.

BODY-39   The Army and Navy lack sufficient space education in their professional development programs, while the Air Force has a separate structure for its space assets.

BODY-40   The US Army and Navy have their own Space Commands, focused on satellite operations and space control. Both branches are considering offensive platforms such as space-based laser systems. The Navy's space program is primarily focused on surveillance for hostile reconnaissance.

BODY-41   The page discusses the Department of Defense's direction to allocate a separate budget for space systems and activities. It highlights the Army's goal of developing its own unique space systems, while also acknowledging the importance of collaboration with other services and agencies. The Navy aims to broaden its involvement in space system development and minimize duplication by leveraging non-navy systems.

BODY-42   The study found that reorganization poses challenges to the Navy's leverage strategy. The Air Force focuses on technical aspects of space operations, while the Army has limited space education and career development programs.

BODY-43   The Navy lacks a comprehensive curriculum on space operations and does not have officers dedicated solely to space. Enlisted sailors can serve in space duty but must return to their original roles afterwards.

BODY-44   The chapter discusses the need for analyzing a situation within the context of national policy objectives and highlights the purpose of the U.S. Commission to Assess United States National Security Space Management and Organization in assessing space capabilities and coordination processes.

BODY-45   The page discusses the potential costs and benefits of establishing an independent military department or corps dedicated to national security space missions, as well as a position of Assistant Secretary of Defense for Space. It compares the current space force situation with that of early air situations to evaluate how well expectations are being met.

BODY-46   The page discusses the conflict between military services and national interests in the employment of new weapons, particularly aircraft. It highlights the need for recognizing when a weapon system may be best employed for the greater good, even if it goes against the interests of a specific service.

BODY-47   The page discusses the debate over space doctrine and the struggle between military services to optimize space capabilities. It highlights the concern that inter-service friction may hinder efforts to maximize the use of space for national interests. The page also draws parallels to historical debates on optimizing new mediums, such as the airplane.

BODY-48   The page discusses the historical neglect and lack of coordination in the development and education of air and space forces, resulting in hindered progress and varying approaches to training. It suggests the need for better integration, standardization, and professional military education in space asset training.

BODY-49   Leadership development in the early British and U.S. air arms was lacking due to entrenched ideas about war. Training for aviation was not seen as different from other specialties, and the need for different types of training was missed. Specialized schools for innovative thinking did not emerge until 1923. The Air Force focuses on pilot-centric education, as pilots lead the Air Force into battle. Other services have multiple weapon types to choose from, but the Air Force primarily relies on its pilots.

BODY-50   The military's lack of emphasis on space and limited education in space studies may hinder progress and development in the field. The Air Force and Army, in particular, have shown a lack of focus on space, while the Navy is attempting to address this issue.

BODY-51   The page discusses the lack of emphasis on space education in the Navy and the organizational issues faced by both countries in organizing their air arms.

BODY-52   The page discusses the organizational structures and command level differences within the military branches regarding space operations. It also highlights the challenges faced in achieving efficiency in materiel development, particularly in aviation, due to conflicting designs, procurement practices, and competition for funds.

BODY-53   The Air Force has been named the executive agent for space, causing tension with other services. The Navy plans to expand its participation in space programs outside of DoD, while the Army recognizes the need to fund its own efforts. Streamlining procurement efforts is necessary for coordinated acquisition of space capabilities.

BODY-54   During World War I, the British and U.S. faced challenges in developing and training their aviation units due to competition, neglect, and a lack of professional development. This resulted in shortages and delayed the realization of aviation's potential as a weapon.

BODY-55   The services treat space career fields differently, with the Air Force having a primary career field, the Army creating a functional area, and the Navy treating it as a sub-specialty. All services lack curriculum devoted to space in professional military education and could do better in preparing their cadres.

BODY-56   The current structure of space forces is not optimal for the nation's needs. The report recommends recognizing space as a top national security issue and merging disparate space activities to ensure funding and dominance in space.

BODY-57   The relationship between the SECDEF and Director of the CIA is crucial for developing and deploying space capabilities. It is important for the US to invest in science and technology resources to maintain its lead in space. The current National Security Space Policy addresses DoD's responsibilities in areas such as launch systems, military applications, and acquiring space weapons systems. The

	situation in space resembles the early development of air power components in the 20th century.
BODY-58	*The current structure of the US military does not support the development of a Military Space Culture. To better prepare for space threats, the US should maintain inter-service cooperation and oversight while keeping the Air Force as the executive agent.*
BODY-59	*The page discusses the need for coordination and reorganization of space capabilities within the Department of Defense to ensure interoperability and efficiency. It suggests the creation of a Space Force and a division of responsibilities similar to the 1947 USAF split.*
BODY-60	*A bibliography of various books and articles related to air force history, space power, and military procurement.*
BODY-61	*This page lists various documents and websites related to the U.S. Air Force, Army, Navy, and government's space policies and operations.*
BODY-62	*The page discusses the struggle for Air Force independence from 1943-1947.*

Notable Passages

BODY-3   "The author finds that we are at a defining moment in history with regard to U.S. aerospace dominance. The transition of space from a war-enabling medium to a war-fighting medium is upon us. With this realization, he concludes that the current national space structure is hampering development of U.S. space forces that could allow potential adversaries to close the capabilities gap. If the U.S. is to maintain its lead, it should soon move to separate space forces along the same model as that of the creation of the USAF in 1947."

BODY-5   "The emergence of independent air forces around the world in the 20th century is unique in that it signified the first time in history that nations had to decide to forcibly separate war-fighting mechanisms, theories and command structures as well as develop completely new doctrine."

BODY-6   "Currently there is an ongoing battle in the upper echelons of the USAF over the 'right mix' of air and space forces. The argument goes beyond inter-service funding battles, as many have suggested renaming the Air Force to the 'Air and Space Force' or the 'Space and Air Force' as a reflection of a natural evolution of its war fighting capabilities, much like the creation of the U.S. Army Air Service, which then evolved through the U.S. Army Air Corps, U.S. Army Air Forces and finally into the U.S. Air Force."

BODY-7   "Similar to Douhet before them, they claim that failure to act now to create a separate U.S. Space Force could allow potential enemies to close the capabilities gap and be as serious a detriment to optimizing U.S. war-fighting capabilities as a further delay in the creation of the USAF might have been at that time."

BODY-8   Using this rational for comparison and considering current U.S. Air Force Effects-Based Operations (EBO), this paper will explore current space capabilities, current and emerging space doctrine and future desired capabilities with those of the U.S. Air Force concept of space operations. This method should offer a solution to the debate over a separate Space Force. If the exploration of this subject produces a negative answer, it should be able to identify conditions to watch for that once set, would signal that the situation was ripe for creation of a fourth independent service for the United States to optimize its future war-fighting capabilities.

BODY-9   "The motivation for requesting such a study in the first place underscored some deep-seated issues that Britain was attempting to come to terms with regarding this new weapon of the air. The German attacks against England's cities in World War I had come as a psychological blow to the British in two respects. First, it violated the sense of security that came with being an island nation protected by the sea and second, as the great sea power of the time, it challenged their traditional beliefs."

BODY-10   "These attacks also brought out the notion that unlike ground and sea warfare, when applying airpower, it was the offense that was the inherently stronger form of war. It certainly appeared better to attack the enemy's air assets while they sat en-mass on the ground than to try to destroy them one by one in the air."

BODY-11   "The World War I experiences had shown the British airmen that unless the aircraft were used in an inherently offensive and strategic role and some sort of unity of command existed; the ability of the air arm to affect the outcome of battles was limited if not totally wasted. This stronger offensive form of war was a major break from the traditional concepts of the Army and Navy and would convince a future airpower advocate, Hugh Trenchard, that change was needed."

BODY-12	"His experiences had convinced him that the airplane, particularly the bomber was unique in its ability to strike directly at the enemy's will by bypassing both the fielded forces and commerce aspect of the economy, and instead strike directly at a country's manufacturing base, in a concentrated manner so as to achieve the desired effect against both the enemy's will and ability in the shortest time possible."
BODY-13	"Due to the lack of funding and general neglect of the air arm, the solving of important tactical problems such as the accurate observation and direction of artillery shells was left to be worked out in the field, often under combat conditions at the front. The larger aims of offensive operations such as bombing and aerial combat were in an even less developed state with little or no guidance from above."
BODY-14	"Naval airmen, confined within the institutional strait-jacket placed on them in 1915-16, turned their backs on naval careers and when the opportunity arose left for the Royal Air Force in large numbers."
BODY-15	"Leader development would be crucial if the air arm were to achieve its full potential."
BODY-16	"The military wing is a success largely because it has been developed and trained as a branch of the army and with the military objects strictly in view. The naval wing is a failure because it has not been designed for naval objects with the result that it has degenerated into a crowd of highly skilled but ill-disciplined privateersmen. What is wanted is to make the naval wing more 'naval' not more 'aerial'." (Asquith Papers quoted in Cooper, 38)
BODY-17	"The success he achieved by combining squadrons under a single command and using them to first gain air superiority and then to attack deeper targets, proved what would become some basic tenets of air power. Most important, he showed that massing of air in order to generate effects across the battlefield was the preferred method of employment and that this could not be accomplished as long as air units were assigned to ground unit commanders."
BODY-18	"You are asking me to fight the battle this year with the same machines as I fought it last year. We shall be hopelessly outclassed, and something must be done…"
BODY-19	"The Army's short-sightedness in not developing separate specialties for aviation meant that most aviation-affiliated men, especially the enlisted force, had been drawn from other branches and considered their tours in aviation to be passing events and experimental and thus not worthy of their full devotion."
BODY-21	"But the fight had been much longer than that waged in Britain, and just as bitter."
BODY-22	"Experiments conducted in the U.S. before its entry into the World War I showed indications that aircraft would not be relegated to observation roles for long, but instead would prove to be a vibrant new weapon."
BODY-23	"Air superiority is a prerequisite for successful air operations. The most effective means to achieve air superiority is through a determined offensive against enemy air forces. Air attacks against enemy air forces and his rear areas, especially when conducted simultaneously, will provide a marked decrease in enemy air action against friendly front lines. Limiting air activity to reconnaissance and observation failed to fully utilize its war-making potential. Battle in the air arm was more effective when concentrated under a single command."
BODY-24	"To enhance the effectiveness of the scouting fleet (cruisers and destroyers) through extended range reconnaissance. To enhance the main battle fleet (battleships and destroyers) through reconnaissance, spotting of shot falls and to defend against

	enemy carrier aircraft. Through attack, slow enemy battleships to allow our battleships to catch and sink them."
BODY-26	"There was a clear need for integration and coordination before a coherent air policy could emerge."
BODY-28	"We do not consider...that air power...has yet demonstrated its value-certainly not in a country situated as ours-for independent operations of such a character as to justify the organization of a separate department."
BODY-29	"any work we do is based on the effect it has on the Anny's operations...No well-defined policy of independent operations by an air force acting independently of the Anny is being developed under present conditions."
BODY-31	"In fact, a series of committees and board convened in the early to mid twenties arrived at essentially the same conclusions; that the lack of a coordinated, effective air procurement program had reduced the U.S. aircraft industry as well as the air ann itself to below a minimum effective level."
BODY-32	"The Army's failure to induct airmen and its policy to assign soldiers from line units to aviation as a tour of duty, meant that the vast majority of airmen had initially been trained in other branches. This created resentment among these former line-officers over being placed under command of a signal corps officer during this tour. The Army had yet to groom a pure airman in a similar manner to which it created specialists in other fields, and the shortage of field grade officers and enlisted men fully versed in airpower created an atmosphere of apathy."
BODY-33	"Continued low priority of the air arms by the respective services would seriously hinder the full realization of air power during the upcoming war."
BODY-34	"Desert Storm has been called 'the first space war', but compared to our space capabilities today, it seems almost equivalent to comparing U.S. airpower participation in World War I to the airpower in Desert Storm."
BODY-35	"The Air Force had been moving toward developing war-fighting capabilities in and from space, but it has since accelerated the effort, as it has become increasingly clear that potential adversaries have recognized space as a U.S. vulnerability and will attempt to exploit it during a conflict."
BODY-36	"The Anny's role in space is in direct support of the land forces and that success in future operations will depend on Anny access to civil, military, allied and commercial space assets."
BODY-37	"The Panel senses erosion in the effectiveness of the DoN's space strategy as evidenced by diffused management responsibilities, failure to participate in requirements formulation for some systems of high potential utility to the Navy and Marine Corps, irregular and decreasing Navy support of space technology and demonstrations, and lack of integrated management of the human resources that form the space cadre."
BODY-38	"The Army recognizes the need for its future leaders to be able to integrate the four operational domains of land, air, sea and space into plans and to understand the unique threats."
BODY-41	"The Anny's main goal is to develop and deploy systems that enhance terrestrial capabilities. While it acknowledges the need to work with other services and national agencies to maximize capability and minimize duplication, it accepts that there are desired capabilities unique to the Anny that will not be filled by national or other service space systems and that it will need to field these systems itself."

BODY-45 "Congress clearly has ideas about what the nation expects from its space forces. By comparing the current space force situation with that of the early air situations, using the DTLOMS criteria of force development, it is possible to reach some sort of conclusion as to how well those expectations are being met."

BODY-46 "That is, for those services to recognize when a new weapon system is best employed in a manner that may not be in their best interest, but is in the interest of the greater good; the interest of the country that they serve. To resist doing so would be wildly irresponsible and unethical on the part of the military."

BODY-47 "In the final analysis, it comes down to what effects are trying to be achieved and which objectives they serve. Doctrinal development should be done while keeping in mind that it is more efficient and more ethical to employ assets in a way that create desired effects as close to the source as possible if national goals are to be met."

BODY-48 "The largest casualty of the above deficiencies appears to be the development of space-power thought. The lethargic attempts to stimulate this area are indicative of poor professional military education for space forces, deep-seated doctrinal beliefs and differing space force structures that allow varying degrees of integrated training and exercises. It appears that a more universal training curriculum would better serve the needs of the nation by ensuring better interoperability and standardization of space asset training."

BODY-49 "The entrenched ideas about war held the senior ranking officers in both countries and both services hostage and made it difficult for them to envision the full potential of aviation."

BODY-50 "It is only natural to assume that space would also be viewed from the Air Force culture as being in a supporting role. In doing so, it is possible that the necessary vision to develop capabilities to fight in and from space would be lacking, since space would be relegated to second-class citizen status."

BODY-51 "Without a serious reconsideration of the PME systems of the services, it is doubtful that military leaders will develop an appreciation for space power or that they will be able to develop the concepts of operation needed to ensure its maximum potential."

BODY-53 "Like the British developments during World War II and the U.S. experience between the wars, the U.S. may be caught in a situation of uncoordinated acquisition efforts for its space capabilities. Some way to streamline and coordinate procurement efforts would better enhance development and fielding of space assets to meet the nation's security requirements."

BODY-54 "The result was that in addition to a general man shortage, aviation faced resistance from other branches, especially in the tight manning environment that existed later in the war. The airmen that the services did manage to develop showed a lack of commitment to their aviation units due to the temporary nature of that tour. No attempt was made to professionally develop airmen by exposing them to the latest thoughts on employment of aviation."

BODY-55 "In many ways, the divergent ideas about space cadre development today closely resemble that faced by both Britain and the U.S. regarding aviation in the first half of the last century. Regardless of the service perspectives on space, it is obvious that they all could do a better job of preparing their cadres to be better space advocates."

BODY-56 "Current and rapidly expanding U.S. dependence on space and the resulting vulnerability demand that space be recognized as a top national security issue. Only with Presidential leadership can commercial, civil, defense and intelligence space sectors work to ensure U.S. dominance in space."

BODY-57 "Investment in science and technology resources, including people, is essential if the U.S. is to maintain its lead in space."

BODY-58 "Any actions or decisions that do not protect the joint nature of our space forces...would cause irrevocable harm to the services' warfighting capabilities. The increased responsibility and authority given to the Air Force....must be balanced by increased oversight from the commander in chief of US Space Command, the Joint Chiefs of Staff, and OSD. Without this oversight, there is potential that space could become focused on support to a single service, its style of warfighting, and to its priorities. This would be contrary to the best interests of the Army."

BODY-59 "In summary, we are on the cusp of a major shift in war-fighting capability, as space begins to transition from an enabling medium to a full-blown battlespace. As this occurs, the United States needs to reorganize its forces to ensure that its space capabilities develop in line with its national objectives. Experience has shown that failure to do so at the appropriate time only delays required force development efforts that are necessary before a mature service can emerge to serve the nation."

A Fork in the Path to the Heavens:
The Emergence of an Independent Space Force

A Monograph
by
Major Jeffrey R. Swegel
USAF

School of Advanced Military Studies
United States Army Command and General Staff College
Fort Leavenworth, Kansas
AY 01-02

Approved for Public Release; Distribution is Unlimited

SCHOOL OF ADVANCED MILITARY STUDIES

MONOGRAPH APPROVAL

Maj Jeffrey R. Swegel, USAF

Title of Monograph: A Fork in the Path to the Heavens, The Emergence of an Independent Space Force

Approved by:

_____ Monograph Director
COL James K. Greer, MMAS

_____ Professor and Director
Robert H. Berlin, Ph.D.   Academic Affairs,
                                            School of Advanced
                                            Military Studies

_____ Director, Graduate Degree
Philip J. Brookes, Ph.D.   Program

Abstract

A Fork in the Path to the Heavens: The Emergence of an Independent Space Force by Major Jeffrey R. Swegel, USAF, 54 pages.

The issues confronted by Britain and the U.S. early in the last century regarding their emerging air power capabilities were hotly debated, and the final decisions for the creation of independent Air Forces was made based on several factors, not all of which have been sufficiently explored. In the same way today, due to its huge technological advantages, the United States faces a difficult decision with regard to its space forces. The arguments for or against creation of an independent space force all have merit, but the final decision will have lasting impact on national defense.

This monograph examines the current environment with regard to United States space capabilities in an attempt to determine when, if ever, the nation should create an independent service for space. To do this, it uses the U.S. Army concept of Force Development to analyze the Doctrine, Training, Leadership, Organization, Materiel and Soldier (DTLOMS) development processes.

First it evaluates the concepts and programs of Britain and the United States during their attempts to come to terms with early 20th century emerging air power capabilities. This sets the framework for the reader and provides insight into the reasons why separation of the air arm was necessary if those nations were to maintain their warfighting capabilities.

Once the groundwork is laid by looking at early air power, an examination of current U.S. Army, Navy and Air Force policies toward their respective services' space cadres is made using the same DTLOMS criteria to determine the effectiveness of each service's approach.

Finally, by comparing the air power and space situations, and placing the latter within current U.S. national security objectives, it makes a judgment as to the effectiveness of the current space structure. The author asks if national interests would best be served by creation of an independent service now, and if not, what conditions could present themselves that would cause the national needs to best be served by the creation of a separate service.

The author finds that we are at a defining moment in history with regard to U.S. aerospace dominance. The transition of space from a war-enabling medium to a war-fighting medium is upon us. With this realization, he concludes that the current national space structure is hampering development of U.S. space forces that could allow potential adversaries to close the capabilities gap. If the U.S. is to maintain its lead, it should soon move to separate space forces along the same model as that of the creation of the USAF in 1947.

TABLE OF CONTENTS

TABLE OF CONTENTS	1
INTRODUCTION	2
EMERGENCE OF THE ROYAL AIR FORCE	6
Doctrine	7
Training	9
Leadership	10
Organization	12
Materiel	14
Soldiers	15
CREATION OF THE U.S. AIR FORCE	18
Doctrine	19
Training	22
Leadership	23
Organization	25
Materiel	27
Soldiers	29
CURRENT CONCEPTS OF SPACE	31
Doctrine	32
Training	34
Leadership	35
Organization	36
Materiel	37
Soldiers	39
A COMPARISON AND ANALYSIS	41
Doctrine	42
Training	44
Leadership	46
Organization	48
Materiel	49
Soldiers	51
CONCLUSIONS AND RECOMMENDATIONS	53
BIBLIOGRAPHY	57

CHAPTER ONE

INTRODUCTION

Although the formal, that is bureaucratic, creation of various nations' navies and armies occurred at distinctive periods in time, the capabilities of man to fight on the land or on/from the sea had existed for millennium by the time countries got around to officially sanctioning and funding their existence as military arms of the State.

However, the emergence of independent air forces around the world in the 20th century is unique in that it signified the first time in history that nations had to decide to forcibly separate war-fighting mechanisms, theories and command structures as well as develop completely new doctrine. This is because the capability to fight in the third dimension hadn't existed, with any degree of effectiveness at least, until the very end of the 19th century and not with controllable, heavier than air machines until the 20th century.[1]

Although the arguments for independent air arms that were made by airpower advocates such as Douhet, Mitchell, Slessor and Trenchard are well known in air forces, little has been written that explains the disparity in rationale and time between the creation of separate air forces such as the Royal Air Force in the United Kingdom in 1918 and that of the U.S. Air Force in 1947.

This near 30-year difference cannot be explained by mere monetary arguments, as the United States was surely in a better financial position to create a separate air arm in the early 1900s than Great Britain. Possibly due to the longer British experience in World War I, they realized a need for certain wartime effects; or perhaps it was due to an earlier and more robust dedication of resources to the endeavor, which led them to the realization of air capabilities.

---

[1] Balloons were used extensively as early as the Mexican-American war, and although in the later battles,

Whatever the reason, the two rationales have not been sufficiently compared in an attempt to discover some common threads that might reveal what conditions set the stage for separation of capabilities into their own command, organization, acquisition and employment structure. Finding that rational may be critical to optimizing the future employment methods of space assets by the United States.

Currently there is an ongoing battle in the upper echelons of the USAF over the "right mix" of air and space forces. The argument goes beyond inter-service funding battles, as many have suggested renaming the Air Force to the "Air and Space Force" or the "Space and Air Force" as a reflection of a natural evolution of its war fighting capabilities, much like the creation of the U.S. Army Air Service, which then evolved through the U.S. Army Air Corps, U.S. Army Air Forces and finally into the U.S. Air Force. Indeed, there is now an almost universal use of the term "aerospace force" in place of simply Air Force.[2]

Yet others, perhaps fearful of more competition for funding and loss of control over assets, have argued that the current structure of a U.S. Space Command and service component commands is a sufficient and effective blend in war fighting capabilities at this point in time. Advocates on both these sides agree that the Air Force is the proper place for the preponderance of space assets due to the similar three-dimensional nature of their use and the inherent strategic effect they can achieve, as well as the heavy reliance on space capabilities by air assets relative to the amount of use by the U.S. Army and Navy. In fact, the Air Force has taken the lead in this respect having nearly 50 and 80 times the number of personnel in its component command, the Air Force Space Command (AFSPC) as exist in the Army and Navy component commands respectively and 40 times as many as in the warfighting command, United States Space Command

---

bombs were dropped, their main purpose was for observation.
[2] Curiously, General Jumper, CSAF, in a speech to the Air Force Association in Dec '01, purposely reverted to "Air and Space Forces", shunning the term "aerospace forces" that had become commonplace in the

(USSPACECOM); it devotes 40 and 19 times the amount of money to AFSPC as the Army and Navy respectively (38 times as much as USSPACECOM's budget) and has co-located the AFSPC Headquarters with USSPACECOM at Peterson AFB, Colorado.[3]

Finally, a third and more presumably progressive camp makes the argument that space is a unique environment and offers distinct challenges regarding access, methods of maneuver, employment and force protection that can only be fully understood by someone educated in the culture to become a "space advocate". Similar to Douhet before them, they claim that failure to act now to create a separate U.S. Space Force could allow potential enemies to close the capabilities gap and be as serious a detriment to optimizing U.S. war-fighting capabilities as a further delay in the creation of the USAF might have been at that time.

This monograph will review the military situations as seen by Great Britain and the United States and make comparisons to establish reasons that led to their respective decisions to establish separate air forces.

To do this, it will use as a framework the U.S. Army concept of Force Development.[4] Thus it will examine Doctrine, Training, Leadership, Organization, Materiel and Soldiers (DTLOMS) using the standard U.S. Army definitions of each as follows:[5]

(1) *Doctrine development.* The process that develops and documents doctrine, tactics, techniques, and procedures for military operations in publications such as field manuals.

(2) *Training development.* The process that produces programs, methods, publications, and devices to support individual and unit training.

1990s.
[3] Air Force Magazine Staff, "2001 Space Almanac," Air Force Magazine 84, no. 8 (August 2001): 28-57.
[4] US Army FM 100-11
[5] US Army War College Staff, How the Army Runs, A Senior Leader Reference Handbook 2001-2002, (Pittsburgh: Government Printing Office, 2001), ch 2.

(3) *Leader development.* The process that produces programs for the training and the professional and personal development of competent and committed leaders for the Army.

(4) *Organizational development.* The process that translates organizational requirements into organizational models and force structure.

(5) *Materiel development.* The process that conceives, develops, and executes solutions to materiel requirements.

(6) *Soldier development.* The process or processes that concern the determination, addition, deletion, or modification of the Army occupational specialties. These range from the development of proposals affecting the force and/or grade structure of existing occupational specialties to the creation of entirely new occupational specialties to accomplish assigned missions.

Using this rational for comparison and considering current U.S. Air Force Effects-Based Operations (EBO), this paper will explore current space capabilities, current and emerging space doctrine and future desired capabilities with those of the U.S. Air Force concept of space operations. This method should offer a solution to the debate over a separate Space Force. If the exploration of this subject produces a negative answer, it should be able to identify conditions to watch for that once set, would signal that the situation was ripe for creation of a fourth independent service for the United States to optimize its future war-fighting capabilities.

CHAPTER TWO

EMERGENCE OF THE ROYAL AIR FORCE

The genesis of the Royal Air Force lay with the November 1911 British Government's order charging the Imperial Defence Committee with the task of "considering the future development of Aerial navigation for naval and military purposes and to suggest measures to secure an efficient aerial Service for the country."[6] The Defence Committee immediately created a sub-committee, to be chaired by Lord Haldane and tasked them to research the matter. In its final report, the Haldane Committee recommended the creation of an aeronautical service as a separate military formation to be named "The Flying Corps" and which was to consist of a military wing (RFC, Military Wing), a naval wing (RFC, Naval Wing) and a central flight training school.[7] The Imperial Defence Committee approved the recommendations in April 1912 and established the "Royal Flying Corps" as a separate military formation.

Although this action helped alleviate some of the problems that plagued British airpower at the time, it did not go far enough and in fact, as we shall see, for various reasons the government even had difficulty implementing all the committee's recommendations. The motivation for requesting such a study in the first place underscored some deep-seated issues that Britain was attempting to come to terms with regarding this new weapon of the air. The German attacks against England's cities in World War I had come as a psychological blow to the British in two respects. First, it violated the sense of security that came with being an island nation protected by the sea and second, as the great sea power of the time, it challenged their traditional beliefs and

---

[6] Chaz Bowyer, History of the RAF, (London: Bison Books Limited, 1977), 12.
[7] Ibid.

methods of waging commerce warfare. These problems were not completely solved until 1 April 1918 with Royal proclamation of the establishment of the British Royal Air Force (RAF).[8]

Doctrine

Both the Royal Navy and the British Army had attempted to employ their meager aviation assets to maximize their effectiveness; for the most part their thinking was severely hampered by each organization's deeply ingrained thoughts about warfare. The British Army had primarily employed their aircraft in support of the front lines, acting as observers, intelligence gatherers and bombers of enemy troop positions and trenches. The Royal Navy had employed their assets in a wholly fleet defense role, either using their aircraft to ward off enemy aircraft or to attack the enemy's gun emplacements on land so as to negate their effect on British ships.[9] Neither service had given consideration to using aircraft in more strategic-effects roles and had only differentiated aerial combat when necessary to defend either individual aircraft or forward based airfields. These parochial policies resulted in Germany's ability to carry out two separate attacks on London, one on 13 June and another on 7 July 1917.[10] Gotha bombers were able to bomb with impunity and virtually without any interference from either the RFC or the RNAS.

These attacks also brought out the notion that unlike ground and sea warfare, when applying airpower, it was the offense that was the inherently stronger form of war. It certainly appeared better to attack the enemy's air assets while they sat en-mass on the ground than to try to destroy them one by one in the air. At the time, air defenses were relegated to the infantryman's rifle, searchlights, possibly some artillery and the occasional fighter that was able to

---

[8] Authorization for establishment of the RAF was actually given with passage of the Air Force (Constitution) Act in November, 1917. Passage of the act did not create an independent Air Force, it only authorized King George to do so, which he did in March the following year, effective 1 April. Bowyer, 37.
[9] Malcolm Cooper, The Birth of Independent Air Power (London: Allen and Unwin, 1986), 6.
[10] Bowyer, 34-35.

scramble in time to fend off an attack. At least until near the end of the First World War, the lack of advanced warning and long start-engine, taxi, takeoff and climb (SETTOAC) times made air intercepts rare unless the defending aircraft was already airborne at the time the attacker arrived. Usually, the attacker had dropped his bombs and was on his way back to friendly territory before the defender could get his machine to engagement altitude.

Throughout all, although aircraft were used offensively in the close fight, the Army and Navy continued to prefer a defensive posture with regard to their own air assets as well as toward England's cities.

Of the two services, the Army was the first to incorporate its aviation into a field formation as a battalion of the Royal Engineers early in 1911, and further divided it into two companies, one of airships and one of airplanes.[11] However, even within a single service, the Army's lack of understanding of the capabilities of these drastically different weapons and its inability to prioritize one or the other led to a lack of any coherent doctrine for the use of either.

The World War I experiences had shown the British airmen that unless the aircraft were used in an inherently offensive and strategic role and some sort of unity of command existed; the ability of the air arm to affect the outcome of battles was limited if not totally wasted. This stronger offensive form of war was a major break from the traditional concepts of the Army and Navy and would convince a future airpower advocate, Hugh Trenchard, that change was needed.

Because of his experiences as a commander on the continent, Trenchard began to see that the traditional ways of waging war were changing. He, as many early airmen, went back to basics in the Clausewitzian sense. He reasoned that if the goal of war was to get the enemy to submit to your will, you had two options. You could either attack his ability to resist or you could attack his will to resist. Traditionally, the role of the Army had been to affect the enemy's ability

---

[11] Bowyer, 12.

to resist, that is to attack the enemy's forces, while the Navy's traditional role was to affect the enemy's will to resist by attacking his commerce through blockades and thus eventually affect his economy.[12] Both of these methods worked but neither was particularly fast and in fact, in the case of equally matched opponents as was the case in World War I, they would eventually lead to unimaginable carnage.

Trenchard reasoned that if an enemy was to be subdued, the faster the better and more humane for both sides. His experiences had convinced him that the airplane, particularly the bomber was unique in its ability to strike directly at the enemy's will by bypassing both the fielded forces and commerce aspect of the economy, and instead strike directly at a country's manufacturing base, in a concentrated manner so as to achieve the desired effect against both the enemy's will and ability in the shortest time possible. Yet the traditions and nature of land and sea war were mismanaging this new asset.

Growing ever more frustrated by what he saw as this inappropriate use of airpower, Trenchard became more and more convinced that the answer lay in the formation of an independent service. As he saw it, it had become an issue of Doctrine.

Training

The training of British aviators just prior to and during most of the First World War was service-specific, steeped in the doctrinal beliefs of each and was performed at separate locations. Even after the Haldane commission's recommendation of a central flying school was enacted, the Royal Navy continued to train the preponderance of their pilots at their own facility; despite sending instructors and some students to the central flight school.[13]

---

[12] Phillip S. Meilinger, The Paths of Heaven, the Evolution of Airpower Theory (Maxwell AFB: Air University Press, 1997), 41-42.
[13] Bowyer, 14-15.

Formal schooling was confined to the technical aspects of how the machines functioned mechanically and aeronautically. There was no formal instruction on the concepts of how to employ the aircraft within its military/naval formation or on the emerging lessons of how to achieve better effects in order to meet the higher commander's intent. Training was focused on how to best employ the machines to support the formations that they were attached to and not how to achieve effects on their own.

Due to the lack of funding and general neglect of the air arm, the solving of important tactical problems such as the accurate observation and direction of artillery shells was left to be worked out in the field, often under combat conditions at the front. The larger aims of offensive operations such as bombing and aerial combat were in an even less developed state with little or no guidance from above.[14] There appears to have been no inclusion in military exercises nor was the air arm effectively integrated into any combat planning beyond that of the lowest ground commanders'.

Formal professional military education was confined to the officers' original branches, if they had served in positions prior to aviation, or to the Army staff college, which provided little instruction on the employment of this new weapon.

Leadership

Senior leaders played an important part in stifling cooperation between the services' aviators. Though there is evidence that shows fairly good relationships between the airmen of the two services themselves, the farther up the chain of command one looks the more one finds not only parochial views toward each service's air assets but also the ingrained attitudes of that service with regard to war and war fighting concepts.

---

[14] Cooper, 29.

Even Trenchard, later a powerful advocate of an independent air arm and the benefits of long range bombing, remained predominantly a soldier throughout the war. Although frustrated with what he saw as a lack of coherent, combined effort on the part of airpower, his views during the war were confined to that of the tactical battlefield and the effects that could be achieved in support of the army's front lines.[15]

For the part of the RNAS, the senior Admiralty was so locked into its Naval concepts of war that as late as 1915 they had failed to organize their aircraft into fighting units of squadrons, preferring instead to position individual aircraft at different locations. This fact is a testament to their lack of understanding of the proper employment of airpower and their Naval mindset in considering each individual aircraft as a ship, rather than form them into mobile combat-effective units such as squadrons.[16]

Though most of this can be attributed to the lack of time for the services to have groomed air minded leaders, the fact remains that few senior leaders in either service were visionary enough to understand and take advantage of the emerging capabilities. There were even fewer who understood the need to begin to experiment with the weapon and the importance of generating open debate in various institutions, such as the staff college, that would be needed before the true nature of air power could be understood. This presence of such parochial, doctrinally steeped leaders only served to exacerbate the problem from both service's airmen's points of view. This became particularly bad in the RNAS, as illustrated by Cooper, in *The Birth of Independent Airpower*, who writes: "Naval airmen, confined within the institutional strait-jacket placed on them in 1915-16, turned their backs on naval careers and when the opportunity arose left for the Royal Air Force in large numbers."

---

[15] Ibid, 24.
[16] Bowyer, 19.

For all their success in their respective services, the need to generate leaders who understood this weapon as well as those employing it had become obvious, and that fact was missed by the vast majority of the leaders of the time. Leader development would be crucial if the air arm were to achieve its full potential.

Organization

Since the invention of heavier-than-air craft, the Royal Navy and British Army each had been experimenting with different blends of airships and aircraft to augment their operations. Each service had its own aviation assets and concepts of operations and employment for each type of craft. Stemming from earlier uses of balloons, the primary roles for all airborne craft were confined to intelligence gathering, surveillance and fire coordination for artillery.

Inter-service rivalry played a significant part in delaying full implementation of the Haldane report's recommendations as the Navy wing (RFC, Navy Wing) preferred to go its own way on aviation matters and eventually even became known as the Royal Naval Air Service (RNAS)[17], leaving the term "Royal Flying Corps" to apply only to the military wing. This significant statement of independence by the Royal Navy probably stemmed from the Navy's resentment of the perceived encroachment on its traditional dominance in military matters. Though there is plenty of blame to be shared by both departments, the resulting lack of coherent national air policy and often competing interests that resulted would become a major factor in late and post World War I arguments.

One of the most telling periods of such inter-service rivalry occurred in 1915 with a dramatic increase of effective German Fokker attacks in France as well as the first effective Zeppelin attacks against London. Until this time, both the Naval Department and the War

---

[17] Bowyer, 14.

Department were insistent on designing their air organizations to be directly in support of their respective objectives and the extent of this parochial thinking is illustrated with the following quote from the (obviously army-leaning) Prime Minister's secretary:

> "The military wing is a success largely because it has been developed and trained as a branch of the army and with the military objects strictly in view. The naval wing is a failure because it has not been designed for naval objects with the result that it has degenerated into a crowd of highly skilled but ill-disciplined privateersmen. What is wanted is to make the naval wing more "naval" not more "aerial". (Asquith Papers quoted in Cooper, 38).

It is true that the Navy had neglected its airmen completely to the point that individual navy airmen took to the development of tactics for employment of naval air and as such, had gained a reputation as rebels and autonomous actors; while the War Department at least had a plan for development of its air arm and had organized along more strict lines. But the point is that despite the secretary's views, the RFC had had little more success in thwarting attacks against England than did the RNAS. In fact, the RFC had as much as admitted defeat in this role by turning over defense of Britain's skies to the RNAS in 1914 while it assumed a role in more direct support of the Army on the continent. The reason for the relative lack of successful German attacks against England during the previous period had more to do with German shortcomings than with successful RFC conduct. However, the above statement illustrates quite well the parochial and misguided thoughts about airpower at the time.

The second and equally important lesson to emerge from the British experience in World War I was the importance of unity of command. As previously mentioned, it was becoming clear that the effects of airpower against the enemy's will to fight were best when applied directly, against the highest level of enemy will and in as great a mass as possible in order to generate maximum shock effect. Similar to the lessons of artillery that were learned in the Americas during the Civil War, the "piece-meal" approach of applying airpower severely limited its benefits.

This was especially true when air resources were assigned to individual field units, as they would tend to be used for the tactical role that best benefited that particular commander. In this way, almost all of the emerging lessons were violated, as it was extremely difficult to achieve mass and strategic effect without air assets being directed by the overall commander to meet his higher intent.

Hugh Trenchard was the first to effectively consolidate air power during the period when he commanded the RFC on the continent. The success he achieved by combining squadrons under a single command and using them to first gain air superiority and then to attack deeper targets, proved what would become some basic tenets of air power. Most important, he showed that massing of air in order to generate effects across the battlefield was the preferred method of employment and that this could not be accomplished as long as air units were assigned to ground unit commanders.

Materiel

The goal of the Imperial Defence Committee's original tasking was to consolidate the country's aviation resources to achieve the efficiency that was perceived to be necessary in order to catch up to other European countries, such as France and Germany, who were more advanced in the field at the time. However, due to the separate services' divergent ideas of aircraft design, procurement and acquisition the situation only worsened. By 1915, the acute problem of supply and acquisition that was being experienced by both the RFC and the RNAS clearly illustrated the need for a centralized system. At one point, the government established a special governmental committee under Lord Derby to resolve this issue of competition for equipment, but he resigned in disgust after only 6 weeks due to the stubbornness of the Admiralty to give in on even the most insignificant of issues.[18]

Another key aspect was the importance and rapidity of technological development on this new weapon. Unlike most traditional naval and military weapons, the aircraft became outdated rapidly and many not directly involved in aviation at the time had trouble understanding the importance of this fact. At one point, frustrated and desperate, Trenchard wrote a note to London stating "You are asking me to fight the battle this year with the same machines as I fought it last year. We shall be hopelessly outclassed, and something must be done…".[19] But the problems of aircraft design and production were not to be solved so easily.

The Army had preferred to use solely standard designs conceived by government engineers and produced at a very limited number of plants. This allowed for more rapid expansion during the war but severely limited the RFC's flexibility in adapting to rapidly changing technology of wartime conditions. The RNAS generally enjoyed a higher quality and broader variety of aircraft but in quantities so small that no manufacturer could ever achieve any sense of production efficiency nor come to count on continuous orders.[20] Overall, it appears that the development of British air power during this period was driven more by a competition between the Navy and Army for funds and prestige than by any operational requirement.

Soldiers

Recruitment was difficult enough during war as the armed services competed with civilian organizations, such as the Ministry of Munitions for skilled labor. It was only made more complicated for the air arms by their inherent need for more technically savvy individuals for both

---

[18] Bowyer, 29.
[19] Hugh Trenchard's Dec 1916 letter to London, quoted by Bowyer, pg 32.
[20] Cooper, 34.

pilots and mechanics. Some of this manpower shortage was alleviated by each service's ability to transfer individuals to their air arms as necessary, but later in the war as the need for officers became even more critical by events on the Western front, branches began to vigorously resist these transfers.[21] The Army's short-sightedness in not developing separate specialties for aviation meant that most aviation-affiliated men, especially the enlisted force, had been drawn from other branches and considered their tours in aviation to be passing events and experimental and thus not worthy of their full devotion.

In addition, there was very little indoctrination done for new arrivals in the way of airpower theory or methods of employment. Most pilots had come from the signal corps or infantry and had their hands full with the technical training aspects of how to fly the dangerous craft of the time and with the mechanical aspects of basic maintenance. The enlisted force had a full time job keeping the unreliable, non-standard aircraft airworthy and showed little enthusiasm for developing a larger view on air power capabilities.

In the RNAS, there were no senior leaders with any aviation experience whatsoever and the Royal Navy aviators had a difficult time explaining the proper employment of the aircraft to London. These Admirals viewed most aviators and their mechanics with distain and thought of them as rebels harboring "anti-navy" sentiments. Such distrust for the troops would be a major cause for the previously mentioned exodus of aviators from the RNAS once the RAF was formed.

This was the situation in Britain from the advent of the airplane until very near the end of the Great War. On 1 April 1918, the British Royal Air Force was a combination of the then existing Royal Flying Corps and the Royal Naval Air Service. But old habits die hard and even after the war the battle raged as both the Army and Navy attempted to re-absorb their respective

---

[21] Cooper, 34-35.

air arms. The Navy was partially successful, eventually re-gaining control over its tactical aviation in the next decade.

CHAPTER 3

CREATION OF THE U.S. AIR FORCE

With the passage of the National Security Act of 1947, Congress created a unified Department of Defense and an independent U.S. Air Force, fulfilling the vision of American airpower advocates that had begun soon after the advent of the Wright Flyer. But the fight had been much longer than that waged in Britain, and just as bitter.

The participation of U.S. air units and individual airmen in World War I had been relatively insignificant as compared to the British. This meant that the preponderance of air employment lessons would never make it back across the Atlantic. Yet the conditions faced by the U.S. Army Air Forces and U.S. Navy during the 1920's, 30's and 40's were similar to those of the British, even if there were some significant differences. They would be studied with similar zeal and as early as the mid 1920's there were indications from such appointed bodies as the Lassiter Board and the Lampert Committee that an independent service might better serve the national interests.[22]

American airpower greats like Billy Mitchell, Carl Spaatz, Benjamin Foulois and Hap Arnold would all wrestle with the same issues that Trenchard had, but within the context of the newfound power and influence of the United States. In particular, Billy Mitchell's background as a privileged son and adventurous young military officer serving in the new territories of an emerging world power would help form his penchant for controversial and independent action. Eventually these experiences would dictate his methods of advocating the possibilities of

---

[22] Herman S. Wolk, The Struggle for Air Force Independence 1943-1947 (Washington DC: Office of Air Force History, 1984), 9.

airpower.[23] The United States would have the advantage of looking back on both good and bad of the British Experience, but it would take experience in another World War and the emergence of our own lessons placed within the context of our own strategic situation before the impetus would exist to create an independent arm.

Doctrine

Experiments conducted in the U.S. before its entry into the World War I showed indications that aircraft would not be relegated to observation roles for long, but instead would prove to be a vibrant new weapon. The problem lay in deciding which aircraft, the fixed wing or the balloon, would dominate. The Navy's problem was further complicated as it had added the seaplane to its repertoire during the Mexican American war, providing yet another choice between ship-borne or sea-borne craft.

Like the Army, the perception of the navy was that airpower was best utilized in support of the surface combatants, in this case navy vessels and in particular, battleships. At the time, the battleship was the major ship of the line and the rest of the fleet was organized around and in support of it. Most naval officers were well steeped in Mahanian doctrine and perhaps even knew the theorist personally; and his ideas about naval warfare would heavily influence their thoughts about the role of airpower as well. Since they believed that control of the seas was a necessary precursor to winning war and the way to achieve that was through a great naval battle, it was logical for them to conclude that the aircraft was another means of supporting that fight.

By the time of U.S. entry into the Great War, the Allies had already established five

---

[23] Mark A. Clodfelter, "Molding Airpower Convictions: Development and Legacy of William Mitchell's Strategic Thought," in The Paths of Heaven, The Evolution of Airpower Theory, ed Meilinger (Maxwell AFB: Air University Press, 1997), 79-114.

principles regarding employment of the air arm that were seemingly well accepted:[24]

1. Air superiority is a prerequisite for successful air operations.

2. The most effective means to achieve air superiority is through a determined offensive against enemy air forces.

3. Air attacks against enemy air forces and his rear areas, especially when conducted simultaneously, will provide a marked decrease in enemy air action against friendly front lines.

4. Limiting air activity to reconnaissance and observation failed to fully utilize its war-making potential.

5. Battle in the air arm was more effective when concentrated under a single command.

The emergence of these agreed upon concepts for the application of air power only tended to strengthen the convictions of Spaatz, Arnold and Foulois. However, due to numerous setbacks in the quest for autonomy over the next 15 years, Army airmen decided to settle for an aviation section divided into two parts; one for tactical application in direct support of ground troops and another more strategic section. During war, this second section would be directly under the overall commander.[25] This arrangement became a reality in 1935 and was a major step toward the Army's acquiescence of the proper application of air.

Like the Army' predominant use of its aviation for observation and spotting, the Navy made substantial gains during the war by learning to employ its aviation against land targets and in the anti-submarine spotting role, but in the case of both services, these were in direct support of their respective surface forces and very little progress was made toward using air assets to achieve battlefield wide effects.

---

[24] Robert T. Finney, History of the Air Corps Tactical School 1920-1940 (Washington DC: Center for Air Force History, 1992), 4.
[25] Richard G. Davis, Carl A. Spaatz and the Air War in Europe (Washington DC: Center for Air Force History,

World War I lessons of the air were largely confined to the Army, since the U.S. Navy hadn't begun aircraft carrier flight operations until the USS Langley in 1922. Consequently, naval air theory and doctrine were largely formed in the years after 1927 with the commissioning of the aircraft carriers USS Lexington and Saratoga[26] and at about the same time as the preponderance of Army Air Corps Tactical School's writings on air theory. Between the wars however, the U.S. Navy began serious experimentation with aviation and began to develop its own ideas on employment.

Several factors helped contribute to the shift in naval thinking about Mahan's great battle, not the least of which was the Five Powers Treaty of 1922. The tonnage and gun size limits placed on countries' battleships by this treaty helped push the development of aircraft carriers, as well as caused a reorganization of the battle fleet from battleship-centric to aircraft carrier-centric. Despite this reorganization, due to Mahanian thought and the reality of the time that ship-borne aircraft could not carry enough bombs to be effective against armored ships, the Navy continued to think of the aircraft as support for the fleet's great battle. In this capacity, they saw three main roles for aircraft:[27]

1. To enhance the effectiveness of the scouting fleet (cruisers and destroyers) through extended range reconnaissance.
2. To enhance the main battle fleet (battleships and destroyers) through reconnaissance, spotting of shot falls and to defend against enemy carrier aircraft.
3. Through attack, slow enemy battleships to allow our battleships to catch and sink them.

1993), 24.
[26] David R. Mets, The Influence of Aviation on the Evolution of American Naval Thought in The Paths of Heaven, (Maxwell AFB, Alabama: Air University Press, 1997) 115.
[27] Ibid, 127.

Like the Army, the Navy realized that a prerequisite to conducting such support operations was command of the air, but the Navy envisioned this to be achieved by disabling or sinking the enemy's aircraft carriers and not by striking the more strategic targets of production and supply. These ideas and the fact that there had not been a single British naval battle fought in WW I in which airpower had been conclusive meant that most naval men perceived aviation as more evolutionary rather than revolutionary.

Training

From the time the Army received its first airplane in 1909 until U.S. entry into World War I in 1917, the Army lacked any formal professional training for the air arm that could be considered comparable to that provided for the other combat arms. Despite the establishment of two flying schools during this period, training stressed only the technical aspects of flying and maintenance. However, through cooperation with civilian agencies and civilian enthusiasts the airmen at these schools conducted unsanctioned, unfunded experiments on many aspects of aviation including mounting machine guns on airplanes, bombing, communication equipment, aerial photography and cooperation with infantry.[28] It is true that the airplane was new and untested in combat and as such it would have been difficult to teach any sort of Tactics, Techniques or Procedures (TTPs) for employment anyway, but what is important to note is the Army's lack of any attempt to formally incorporate the aircraft into training exercises or to experiment with any TTPs during this period.

U.S. Army's neglect of its aviation even during World War I's early days resulted in the United States entering the war without a single aircraft suitable for advanced training or a single

---

[28] Finney, 3.

instructor-qualified pilot. The result was American dependence on European training facilities and aircraft during the American Expeditionary Force (AEF) period.[29]

The Navy's resistance to incorporating its aviation into major exercises until the famous "fleet problems" of the late 1920's illustrated its predominant surface mindset toward battle. Even then, aircraft were not used in any strategic role, but in direct support of the fleet to gain an advantage over the enemy in the great battle that they hoped would achieve command of the sea. There was no coordination with Army ground or air units and no attempt to use airpower to achieve battlefield wide effects that would serve the higher commanders' intent.

The WWI experiences pressed home the need for establishment of a school devoted to the education of airmen. This was accomplished by the War Department in 1920 with the establishment of eleven special service schools for the Air Service, one of which was the Air Service School at Langley Field, Virginia.[30] This school would eventually become the Air Corps Tactical School at Maxwell AFB, Alabama and the fountain of knowledge for employment, training and exercises for the fledgling air arm. Unfortunately, the Navy established no such schools and continued to train its aviators as surface sailors first and specialist airmen second. There was a clear need for integration and coordination before a coherent air policy could emerge.

Leadership

Leadership of the Army during WW I had little opposition to air independence due to the relatively low participation of American air power and the fact that what participation that did happen was mainly relegated to direct support of ground operations. Thus there were few airmen

---

[29] Davis, 5.
[30] Finney, 9.

strongly advocating separation, and those who had come to believe it was needed were of low rank and had little influence.

Between the wars, as the lessons from Britain filtered back across the Atlantic, the question was to be debated as hotly in the United States as it had been in Britain. Individuals like Carl Spaatz, Hap Arnold, Billy Mitchell and Benjamin Foulois would carry the banner against an entrenched Army bureaucracy and some powerful anti-independence leaders including President Roosevelt. However, armed with the experience of the past war, the emerging lessons of ongoing experimentation and with a few key supporters, not the least of which would be General Douglas MacArthur, (who at the time of the creation of GHQ Air Force, was Army Chief of Staff), they would achieve some measure of success.

Carl Spaatz had spent most of his flying career in support of General Pershing's Mexican adventures in 1916. Although his only combat experience in World War I was 4 weeks spent at the front near the end of the war, he had several assignments involving the training and supplying of air units. This extensive experience running the Army's training for airmen and insight on development of air-minded individuals convinced him of the need to develop air specialists.

General Billy Mitchell's background as a signals officer would prove beneficial to the evolving air arm due to the signal corps' emphasis on technology and ingenuity, both of which were needed in the fledgling air arm. Early in his career he had often been stationed in remote and solitary locations and worked without supervision, accomplishing much that others had tried and failed. This fostered the immense self-confidence and proclivity for fierce independent action that would endear him to his followers, estrange him to his detractors and eventually end his career.[31]

---

[31] Clodfelter in Paths of Heaven, 81-82.

Many within the War Department and government in general considered independence unnecessary, simply due to the geographic isolation that the U.S. enjoyed from its oceans. Just prior to General Mitchell's court martial, an incensed President Coolidge, growing tired of the General's rantings, convened the Morrow board to study American aviation. The board concluded that "We do not consider…that air power…has yet demonstrated its value—certainly not in a country situated as ours—for independent operations of such a character as to justify the organization of a separate department".[32] This was the predominant view of most leaders resulting from their service-centric view of airpower and their experiences of World War I. It only underscored the need to develop a cadre that fully understood the potential of the aircraft.

In the meantime, the Navy had its own ideas. The true measure of a sailors worth, whether he was an aviator or not, was his competence in his surface specialty. Though there was a high importance placed on education and experience, the naval officers of the time had witnessed the advent of weapons like the torpedo and submarine, both of which had at one time or another been called "revolutionary", but eventually proved otherwise.[33] As a result, no special schools were started to develop specialists in air employment and the War College's curriculum was not significantly modified to reflect the emergence of this new weapon. Debate over the proper employment of air power was confined to the naval airmen, who at this time, were just beginning to achieve field rank.

Organization

U.S. Army Air Force Organization began in 1907 as the aeronautical division of the signal corps, and in 1914 was established as the aviation section of the signal corps. Later and as a result of the success shown by the newly formed RAF, Congress established the U.S. Army Air

---

[32] Clodfelter, 105.

Service.[34] Having had little participation in World War I, the inter-war years for the U.S. Army Air Service organizational structure was to rely heavily on the lessons learned by British airmen, and in particular the success enjoyed by Hugh Trenchard just prior to and after the RAF gained independence. During this period he had consolidated the air of the British Expeditionary Force under a single commander and employed them in mass, achieving great results on the continent.

Despite this evidence, U.S. Army commanders considered direct support of ground troops as the most useful role for the Air Service and considered strategic application of airpower the realm of dreamers. As such, they reasoned the air should be subordinated to the will of the ground commanders.

In 1925, during testimony to the House of Representative's Lampert Committee, which was investigating U.S. Aviation, Carl Spatz[35] commented, "we follow the doctrines laid down by the Army for their operations so far as the Army is concerned." And added "any work we do is based on the effect it has on the Army's operations…No well-defined policy of independent operations by an air force acting independently of the Army is being developed under present conditions."[36]

Going back to the 1800's, the Navy had been organized into bureaus that made a sharp distinction between "line officers" and "engineer officers" and this policy had caused them many problems in everything from promotions to cooperation.[37] As a result, a command structure change was made in 1915 that created a Chief of Naval Operations (CNO) to decrease the bureau chief's power, increase cooperation and eliminate stove-piping of ideas. The result was

---

[33] Mets, 117.
[34] Wolk, 6.
[35] "Spatz" is the correct spelling of his name at this time. It was not until 1937 that he petitioned the courts to officially change it to "Spaats" in an attempt to correct constant mispronunciation of his name, which is supposed to sound like "spots". Davis, 3.
[36] Davis, 20.
[37] Mets, 124.

greater efficiency of ideas and a general feeling that a sailor best served the navy by gaining competence as a sailor first, and in his specialty second. This idea was deeply entrenched and held for all specialties, save the marines, and was probably the foundation for the stiff resistance to calls for development of a naval air corps.

The U.S. Navy had no aircraft carriers during World War I and had attached individual aircraft, in the form of airships and seaplanes directly to fleets instead of organizing them into squadrons and used them in direct support of surface fleets at the will of the fleet commanders. As stated above, between the wars the Navy had reorganized the battle fleet around the aircraft carrier to avoid restrictions of the Five Powers Treaty, but although the means had changed, it did not significantly affect the idea that the main goal was to gain command of the sea.

Materiel

Prior to WW I, the Wright Brothers had acquired a patent on the aircraft and as a result other designers were forced to make significant, if not radical changes to control designs in order to avoid litigation. There is also evidence to suggest that the U.S. Army signal corps had numerous problems with the quality of Wright aircraft and despite protests, the problems went unfixed. While attempting to use aircraft from different manufacturers with these radically different control designs, the Army experienced significant accident rates as a result of pilot's difficulty in adapting to these differences.[38]

As a result of their attempt to stay out of World War I, Congress was reluctant to fund earlier aviation until it was too late. Upon entering the war, there was not a single aircraft in the U.S. Army inventory capable of advanced training or combat and the few U.S. airmen that would make it into the war would be forced to use European equipment and training facilities. The Navy fared no better as they had trouble prioritizing between their dirigibles, seaplanes or land-based planes and thus never presented a coherent case for funding for any aircraft.

After the war however, U.S. Air Corps' annual budget averaged just over 18 percent of the Army's budget between the years 1920 and 1934.[39] Although this showed a more serious commitment to the development of this new arm, in the post-war fiscal environment it became a source of major friction within the Army.

Procurement was disorganized and a product of geographically separated companies, low demand and excess production due to uncoordinated and irregular orders, differing designs and export controls on technology. A variety of design considerations and erratic funding by both services exacerbated the situation as they competed with demand from overseas and the companies tried to balance that with U.S. export laws. In fact, a series of committees and board convened in the early to mid twenties arrived at essentially the same conclusions; that the lack of a coordinated, effective air procurement program had reduced the U.S. aircraft industry as well as the air arm itself to below a minimum effective level.[40]

By August 1933, the situation had grown bad enough that the Drum board, while trying to plan air support for war plans, was unable to accept a basic assumption for number of aircraft available. It attempted to solve the dilemma by recommending force strengths for the air arms of each service that would be necessary to support current plans, but the results were mixed. The Navy's plan became clear and produced exact numbers, but the Army's plan was so ambiguous that it was easily challenged by Congressional committee.[41]

---

[38] Herbert A. Johnson, Wingless Eagle (Raleigh: University of North Carolina Press, 2001), 3.
[39] Davis, 14.
[40] Irving Brinton Holley, Jr., Buying Aircraft: Materiel Procurement for the Army Air Forces (Washington DC: Center of Military History, 1989), 45-47.
[41] Holley, 54.

On the eve of a second World War, these diverse recommendations indicated the need for a single voice to speak for force development of the nation's air arm.

Soldiers

Even with the limited World War I experiences of the U.S., the most glaring shortcoming in both services was the lack of airmen, officers and enlisted, trained in the employment of air power. Though a glaring deficiency, the more immediate and more pressing problem faced in Europe was the lack of basic flight training school facilities and aircraft. In fact, the Army's low priority on aviation meant that at the time the U.S. entered the war, it had a total of only 65 trained aviators in its ranks. The Army's failure to induct airmen and its policy to assign soldiers from line units to aviation as a tour of duty, meant that the vast majority of airmen had initially been trained in other branches.[42] This created resentment among these former line-officers over being placed under command of a signal corps officer during this tour. The Army had yet to groom a pure airman in a similar manner to which it created specialists in other fields, and the shortage of field grade officers and enlisted men fully versed in airpower created an atmosphere of apathy.

As a partial remedy, the Air Service Field Officer's School was set up at Langley Field in Virginia.[43] Though a major step forward, the intent was still not to create airmen from their induction, as the school was designed as a field officer's course. Also, the Army's initial neglect to incorporate the school into field exercises limited airmen's experience and practical application as well as curtailing the regular Army's exposure to air power. As stated above, the Navy took no action toward recognizing the uniqueness of their air arm and made no significant changes in their Professional Military Education courses that would have stimulated discussion and debate

---

[42] Davis, 10.
[43] Finney, 7-10.

over the role of the new air weapon. Sailors remained sailors first and aviators second. Development of both service's airmen would suffer as a result.

With the onset of World War II the atmosphere had changed enough that at least the services had begun to induct soldiers and sailors directly into their air arms. However, the army once again revealed its short sightedness with respect to the air army by deciding that it could not afford to have its air officers assigned to teaching staffs and closed the Tactical school in June of 1940. However, soon realizing its mistake, in 1942 it opened the Army Air Force School of Applied Tactics in order for airmen to focus on the global problems of airpower with which the U.S. was now faced.[44] Continued low priority of the air arms by the respective services would seriously hinder the full realization of air power during the upcoming war.

---

[44] Finney, 83.

CHAPTER 4

CURRENT CONCEPTS OF SPACE

Upon creation of U.S. Space Command (USSPACECOM) in 1985, the services designated their existing individual space organizations as their respective components for this new war-fighting command. Later in 1986, the Joint Staff and its chairman position were created by the Goldwater-Nichols Act in an attempt to unify war-fighting efforts and streamline the chain of command. Command would now pass from the unified commands through the Secretary of Defense (SECDEF) to the President, instead of through the separate service chiefs, and the Chairman would exercise operational control by passing orders of the President or SECDEF to the Unified Commanders. But unlike the other commands, when dealing with space (and much like dealing with information operations), the lines between when the command is in the supporting versus the supported role are unusually ill-defined, and will continue to blur even more as space capabilities grow in the coming decades.

Desert Storm has been called "the first space war", but compared to our space capabilities today, it seems almost equivalent to comparing U.S. airpower participation in World War I to the airpower in Desert Storm. Space use and capabilities since 1990 have so dramatically increased that much of what was accomplished by all services during the operations in Afghanistan would have been impossible without them. Because of this increasing reliance on space, tension between the services has escalated as they struggle to compete for space money, capabilities and resources.

Further adding to the competitive atmosphere, in May 2001, the DoD named the Air Force as the executive agent for space. While placing significant burdens on the Air Force, it was also viewed as opening vast opportunities. However, it has caused some uneasiness in the other services that depend heavily upon space assets to accomplish their missions. A careful analysis of how the separate services view space, how we as a joint team use space and the frictions between the two may reveal some interesting insight.

Doctrine

The Air Force has incorporated its space thought into its doctrinal thinking as evidenced by Air Force Basic Doctrine (AFDD –1). This document treats space forces in the same manner with which it discusses air forces, using similar terms and applying the Air Force's Tenets of Air Power and Core Competencies to space. The Air Force has also developed a separate document, Air Force Doctrine Document 2-1 (AFDD 2-1), which is the primary Air Force source for space doctrine.

The Air Force view of space encompasses a wide range of missions; offensive, defensive and enabling. AFDD 2-1 discusses roles like defensive counter space, offensive counter space and space superiority, while at the same time recognizing an enabling mission for the war-fighters of the four services as well as for civilian agencies.[45] In this way, it also realizes the need to be able to defend U.S. space assets as well as deny, disrupt and degrade those space assets of our adversaries. This last point is even more important for the Air Force since it was named the DoD executive agent for space.

The Air Force had been moving toward developing war-fighting capabilities in and from space, but it has since accelerated the effort, as it has become increasingly clear that potential adversaries have recognized space as a U.S. vulnerability and will attempt to exploit it during a conflict.

---

[45] Air Force Doctrine Document 2-2 (Maxwell AFB, AL: Air University Press, 1998), 21-24.

The Army does not have a space doctrine per se, but instead deals with space by incorporating space applications into its regular doctrine and promulgating an Army Space Policy. This policy includes support to civilian agencies also, but clearly states that the Army's role in space is in direct support of the land forces and that success in future operations will depend on Army access to civil, military, allied and commercial space assets.[46]

The Army concept of space is to optimize its capabilities in order to enhance traditional Army operations. It also acknowledges that to receive maximum benefits, it must integrate space throughout its actions, activities and units and incorporate it into all exercises and operations.[47]

The Navy, true to form, does not have a published space doctrine, at least not yet. However it does recognize the increasing importance of incorporating space support in its exercises and operations. Its policy is to integrate space into every facet of naval operations, with primary emphasis on providing space-based support to the war-fighter down to the lowest tactical level.[48]

The Naval Doctrine Center has recently made serious attempts at consolidating naval concepts of space operations and is beginning to produce the first publications on naval space thought. These consist of several drafts and some recently published Naval Tactics, Techniques and Procedure (NTTP) publications such as the Naval Space Tactics Manual, the Navy Space Vulnerability Products Guide and Navy Space Handbook.

In spite of the Navy's recent movement toward doctrine development, there are still some serious shortcomings. In a March 2002 completed study by the Center for Naval Analyses, they highlighted some serious weaknesses in the Navy space program. In it they stated:

---

[46] FM 100-18, Space Support to Army Operations, Internet, http://adtdl.army.mil/cgi-bin/atdl.dll/fm/100-18/f0018_1.htm#ref1h2., accessed 15 March 2002.
[47] U.S. Army Space Reference Text, 1993, Internet, http://www.tradoc.army.mil/dcscd/spaceweb/chap4im.htm, accessed 15 March, 2002.
[48] Department of the Navy, SECNAV Instruction 5400.39B, 26 August 1993, Internet,

> "The Panel senses erosion in the effectiveness of the DoN's space strategy as evidenced by diffused management responsibilities, failure to participate in requirements formulation for some systems of high potential utility to the Navy and Marine Corps, irregular and decreasing Navy support of space technology and demonstrations, and lack of integrated management of the human resources that form the space cadre."[49]

It's clear that due to the diverse missions of the services, there are varying views on how space can be used to benefit war-fighting in future conflicts.

Training

The integration of space capabilities has been lacking in general, but the services have been making some progress toward exercising with and planning for space resources. For the first time, the Air Force imbedded hostile force space capabilities into its Red Flag exercise in August 2001, giving the adversarial "red team" the ability to deny friendly forces heavily relied upon space-based capabilities such as Global Positioning Systems (GPS) and secure communications.[50] It has also begun to incorporate space into its annual Future Games through various hostile space scenarios and attempted to derive ways to counter foreseen enemy capabilities and attacks on our space assets, both earthbound and in space. It has developed conceptual space-borne weapons platforms such as "killer satellites" and space-based dazzle lasers that will be able to fight from, and in space itself. There has been a significant increase in use of these capabilities in the Air Force exercises and training events.

The Army has stated a desire to incorporate space applications into its exercises, training scenarios, war games and war plans.[51] For nearly a decade it has been attempting to create

---

http://www.fas.org/spp/military/docops/navy/secnav_inst_5400_39b.htm, accessed 20 March 2002.
[49] Report of the Panel to Review Naval Space, Assured Space Capabilities for Critical Mission Support, Center for Naval Analyses, March 2002, 1.
[50] Red Flag Gets Space-Related Twist, Air Force Magazine, November, 2001, 18.
[51] FM 100-18, Space Support to Army Operations, 1994, Internet, http://adtdl.army.mil/cgi-bin/atdl.dll/fm/100-

general space awareness training and education for individuals and units so that they will be trained and intimately familiar with space weapons and equipment necessary to conduct their missions.[52]

Naval exercises use space assets to a greater degree than the Army. This is driven by the need for distant sea fleets to have information regarding hostile reconnaissance assets and the need to keep communication for command and control. The Navy has stated a desire to exercise its units and personnel using space assets down to the lowest tactical level.[53] Although some progress is being made in this area, the actual tactical document for use of these assets is still in draft at the time of this writing.

Leadership

Pilots, not space specialists, have always commanded USSPACECOM and Air Force Space Command (AFSPC)[54]. This despite the fact that the missile career field has existed for decades and the space career field for more than ten years.

Curriculum at the Air University does not contribute significantly to developing space thinkers. The Air Command and Staff College curriculum contains one core course and two elective courses pertaining to space operations and theory/doctrine development. The War College curriculum contains roughly the same amount of dedication, though on a more national policy level.

The Army recognizes the need for its future leaders to be able to integrate the four operational domains of land, air, sea and space into plans and to understand the unique threats

---

18/f0018_1.htm#ref1h2., accessed 15 March 2002.
[52] U.S. Army Space Reference Text.
[53] Department of the Navy, SECNAV Instruction 5400.39B.
[54] With two exceptions for AFSPC: LtGen Moorman from 29 March 1990 to 23 March, 1992, who had an intel/recce/space background and at the time of this writing, LtGen Lance Lord has been selected as the new

from hostile space capabilities. This realization means that the Army wants leadership programs that develop a robust space capabilities awareness at all levels of the force.[55]

Despite these stated objectives, the Army Command and Staff College does not have a single space course in its core curriculum and as a result, the only exposure to space that Army officers have at that level of professional education is embodied in two electives offered during the year. The Army War College curriculum is little better, devoting its time to the study of National Space policy and its impact on development of the Army's view.

Surface warfare specialists and naval aviators dominate leadership of the Naval Space Commands. The professional development of officers regarding exposure to space is limited in the Naval War College (both the command and the staff course), despite the Secretary of the Navy's now nine-year-old proclamation to develop a cadre of space experts.[56] Although several courses and the opportunity to study space as an academic discipline exist at the Naval Post Graduate school, few naval officers get the opportunity to attend the Post Graduate school and even fewer choose space as their area of concentration.

Organization

Of the three major services, the Air Force was the first to incorporate a separate structure for its space assets. The Air Force officially created its Space Command in 1982 and its mission gradually expanded to include the missileers. AFSPC is a 2-star command directly under HQ/USAF and consists of two Numbered Air Forces (NAFs) and several Space Wings and Missile Wings. This structure closely replicates the Air Force's force-supplier structure for the other mission-oriented unified commands. The space wings provide direct support to all DoD and

---

commander and has a missile background.
[55] U.S. Army Space Reference Text.

U.S. Government agencies as well as two major commands, USSPACECOM, and the North American Aerospace Defense Command (NORAD).[57]

The Army created its Space Command in 1984 as a field element, eventually renaming it as its space command (USARSPACE) in 1988 as a 1-star level command. It is part of the Army Space and Missile Defense Command (SMDC) and it consists of three battalions (one is National Guard) that oversee satellite operations and the space support mission. These missions are heavily oriented toward space control, though the Army is considering the creation of operational requirements documents to justify their entry into the arena of more offensive oriented platforms such as space-based laser systems and the airborne Big Crow system.[58]

Since 1993, the Army has strived to create a hierarchy similar to other branches to clarify responsibility for space proponency in all aspects, including the identification of space positions within Tables of Organization and Equipment (TOE) to support the Army.[59]

The Navy created its Space Command in 1983 and it has grown to over 300 people under the command of a 2-star Admiral. The Navy also operates the alternate Space Control Center for the USSPACECOM's Cheyenne Mountain complex. Though the Navy refers to its space organizations as either detachments or commands, they have not clearly delineated the chain of command and responsibilities for each of its units. Like the Army, the Navy's space program is heavily oriented on space control, especially surveillance in order to keep the fleet informed of hostile reconnaissance.

Materiel

Current Air Force budget allocates approximately nine percent toward space efforts.[60]

---

[56] Department of the Navy, SECNAV Instruction 5400.39B.
[57] The missile wings provide direct support for USSTRATCOM.

Direction by DoD in May 2001 added a separate DoD budget line for space systems and activities. Although as the executive agent, the Air Force has control over spending, it must seriously consider the desired capabilities of the Army, Navy and Marines.

The Army's main goal is to develop and deploy systems that enhance terrestrial capabilities. While it acknowledges the need to work with other services and national agencies to maximize capability and minimize duplication, it accepts that there are desired capabilities unique to the Army that will not be filled by national or other service space systems and that it will need to field these systems itself. It also desires a holistic approach to systems development in that it recognizes that space-based solutions may be cheaper than land-based solutions over the long term and that to maximize this efficiency, it should move now to imbed space technologies in its new equipment acquisitions.

The Navy has stated that it intends to broaden its participation in all aspects of space system development and operation, especially those outside the Navy. It has also recognized the importance of developing, acquiring and supporting the operation of space systems in order to fulfill what it sees as its unique requirements. Importantly, it acknowledges the possibility of duplicating efforts in this endeavor and has vowed to attempt to avoid it by leveraging non-navy systems to the maximum extent.[61]

In light of the DoD decision to implement the Space Commission's recommendations that placed the Air Force as the executive agent for space and reorganized the National Reconnaissance Office, some of these earlier objectives have been called into question by the

---

[58] Interservice Static in Space, Air Force Magazine, Sept 2001.
[59] U.S. Army Space Reference Text.
[60] Spaceflight Now web page, Internet, http://spaceflightnow.com/news/n0004/12afspacebudget, accessed 8 March 2002.
[61] Department of the Navy, SECNAV Instruction 5400.39B.

latest study. In particular, the study found that reorganization posed particular challenges to the Navy's stated "leverage" strategy stated above.[62]

Soldiers

The Air Force created its Air Force Specialty Code (AFSC) for space in the 1990s and it is a primary specialty--as is pilot, navigator or air traffic controller. The Air Force does active recruiting for direct entry into space operations for both officer and enlisted personnel. Although there is some attention paid to space issues at both levels of Air University education, the preponderance is done in specialty schools for space operators and deal more with the technical aspects of space operations than with development of doctrine and policy. Development of enlisted airmen is non-existent except for those in the space career field, and then is focused on technical applications necessary to perform their duties.

The Army's goal throughout the 90's was to create a core of Army space expertise through both education and career development programs that would effectively exploit its use of space and aid in its transformation.[63]

As part of its OPM XXI, the Army recently created Functional Area Forty (FA-40) for its officers desiring a career as space operators. However, it is not a primary branch and officers are encouraged to prepare themselves "to be an FA 40 by first becoming a good, competent Army officer, well-grounded in your branch tactical and technical skills."[64]

Overall, despite the stated desire eight years ago for soldier development programs, there is still very little space education done at the Command and General Staff College and little more

---

[62] Report of the Panel to Review Naval Space, Assured Space Capabilities for Critical Mission Support, Center for Naval Analyses, March 2002, 1.
[63] U.S. Army Space Reference Text.
[64] U.S. Army FA-40 web site, Internet, http://www.smdc.army.mil/FA40/requisite.htm, accessed 15 March, 2002.

at the Army War College.

In 1993, the Navy stated a goal to "develop and advance a cadre of personnel with specialized expertise in space operations and space systems development".[65] Although the Naval Space Command does conduct its own training, it is on those technical aspects necessary for space personnel to accomplish their tasks and it is focused on providing support to the war-fighter. The command further states that it sees itself tasked with four mission areas that include performing essential operations, developing space expertise, advocating naval space requirements and fostering technology.[66] In the broader picture however, the Naval Staff College and War College curriculum devote little time to the evolution of space thought, space operations, doctrine development or theory.

The Navy has sub-specialty codes for officers wishing to broaden into space operations and as such, has no officer cadre with space as their primary concern. Their enlisted sailors from 12 different career specialties can volunteer to serve their shore tour in a space duty billet.[67] These sailors will however, be expected to return to their (presumable sea-going) "rate" upon completion of that shore duty.

---

[65] Department of the Navy, SECNAV Instruction 5400.39B.
[66] U.S. Navy Space Command training web site, Internet, http://www.navspace.navy.mil/training/training.htm, accessed 15 March 2002.
[67] U.S. Navy Space Command career web site, Internet, http://www.navspace.navy.mil/careers/jobs.htm, accessed 15 March, 2002.

CHAPTER 5

A COMPARISON AND ANALYSIS

Any analysis of a situation that could possibly require a cabinet-level reorganization must be done within the context of directed National Policy objectives, much as was done by the British and U.S. governments while attempting to assess air capabilities. Only within this context can it be determined if agencies are performing as intended by the nation's leaders. In this case, Congress attempted to assess U.S. Space capabilities by passing Public Law 106-65.

The National Defense Authorization Act for FY 2000 established the U.S. Commission to Assess United States National Security Space Management and Organization. Its charter was to assess:[68]

1. The manner in which military space assets may be exploited to provide support for United States military operations.

2. The current interagency coordination process regarding the operation of national security space assets, including identification of interoperability and communications issues.

3. The relationship between the intelligence and non-intelligence aspects of national security space…and the potential costs and benefits of a partial or complete merger of the programs, projects or activities that are differentiated by those two aspects.

4. The manner in which military space issues are addressed by professional military education institutions.

---

[68] Report of the Space Commission to Assess United States National Security Space Management and Organization, 11 January 2001, Internet, http://www.defenselink.mil/pubs/spaceintro.pdf, accessed 20 March 2002.

5. The potential costs and benefits of establishing:

   A. An independent military department and service dedicated to the national security space mission.

   B. A corps within the Air Force dedicated to the national security space mission.

   C. A position of Assistant Secretary of Defense for Space within the Office of the Secretary of Defense.

Congress clearly has ideas about what the nation expects from its space forces. By comparing the current space force situation with that of the early air situations, using the DTLOMS criteria of force development, it is possible to reach some sort of conclusion as to how well those expectations are being met.

Doctrine

During the formative years of airpower, England's views on war had been deeply ingrained by centuries of familiarity with land and especially naval warfare. Experiences had been essentially the same for the United States, albeit with less of a history of war. Yet the similar geographic situations as well as the heavy British influence in the U.S. led to the same perceptions within her military.

Attempts by both countries to come to terms with the new heavier-than-air weapon had two dimensions; the national objectives and those of the services. This led to debate over the proper methods of employment in order to receive maximum benefits from this new weapon. Of course, what was meant by "maximum benefits" depended on your point of view.

Nations want to obtain maximum benefits from their investment in their militaries as it pertains to effectiveness and efficiency of winning wars, in order to allow the country to get on with the business of doing business. From their perspective, they want the most effective employment of any new weapon, without regard to how that is done or which organization does it. This puts that interest in possible (though not definite) conflict with that nation's armed services.

From the services' perspectives, it is easy to understand why they would view things differently. They want to achieve maximum effectiveness from any new weapon system as it pertains to helping them achieve victory in the shortest, most efficient manner while still fighting the way they traditionally fight. This in itself is a formula for conflict both between the services themselves and between services' and national desires. From the military's viewpoint, it would be shameful to not use a new weapon to achieve efficiency on the battlefield in order to limit the duration and thus the brutality of war; yet here is still a higher moral issue. That is, for those services to recognize when a new weapon system is best employed in a manner that may not be in their best interest, but is in the interest of the greater good; the interest of the country that they serve. To resist doing so would be wildly irresponsible and unethical on the part of the military.

However, armed only with their historical experiences, both countries' services sought to use the weapon in direct support of its respective forces. At the same time, they missed the fact that this new weapon had abilities to affect warfare like nothing they had ever experienced; indeed, like nothing perhaps since the invention of gunpowder.

It is very evident, that while the military service hierarchies were locked into their historical doctrinal thinking, those directly involved with the air services began to realize the potential of the air weapon. Once that happened, the airmen began the innovative thinking and technological drive that set them apart from their services. Through staunch advocacy and experimentation that would lead to demonstration, they eventually proved their point and became independent services.

Thus, the issue of how best to employ the aircraft became one of great significance, and often put the military at odds with their nations, and airmen at odds with their services. In both cases, this eventually led to the governments ordering studies to determine the means of employment that would best serve national interests.

In this same way, the debate over space doctrine rages today. The individual services wrestle with the most effective means to use the medium of space to increase their own efficiency at war-fighting. This often causes considerable friction between services over capabilities, uses and priorities.

Additionally, this country has become concerned that this inter-service friction and rivalry has slowed its efforts to optimize the use of space. The debate is not only one of which service gets what capability, it is also of how to best develop and employ that capability. This may put the country at odds with its military services, but the country's goals should obviously take priority.

The arguments of the first half of the 20th century are amazingly similar to those being made now. Each service is struggling to optimize space in order to support its way of fighting war. The country is distressed that perhaps this new medium is as revolutionary as the airplane was and the parochial thinking within the military is keeping it from maximizing return on its space investment.

In the final analysis, it comes down to what effects are trying to be achieved and which objectives they serve. Doctrinal development should be done while keeping in mind that it is more efficient and more ethical to employ assets in a way that create desired effects as close to the source as possible if national goals are to be met.

Training

Training during the early years for the air arms of both countries was designed around the flawed doctrine of each service and the governments' late recognition of the strategic capabilities of air power. As such, it was very technical and tactical in nature and intended to develop skills to support their respective forces. Not much thought was given to the development of alternative methods of employment that might have had greater, more strategic effects. Despite this, experimentation was done in all services and by both countries as un-funded, unsanctioned projects of those directly involved with aviation. General neglect of this new weapon led to uncoordinated efforts in the areas of experimentation, exercises and planning that greatly hindered the solving of even tactical problems. The professional military education of early airmen suffered as a result of the services' lack of acknowledgement of their air arms' unique needs and the resultant divergent ideas on how to educate airmen.

The space cadres of today don't suffer quite as badly as those early airmen did, as the relatively recent airpower experience has broadened the minds of the services as well as governments.... but that is not to say there aren't any problems. While all the services do a fairly commendable job of educating their space forces in technical aspects of their jobs, they don't all agree on the proper role for space as it pertains to their interests or to that of their country. As a result, integration in plans, exercises and education vary widely from service to service. The Air Force is probably the most advanced at incorporating all aspects of space into its training and exercises, but it is doing so more than a decade after such capabilities first existed. The Army and Navy are just now realizing the need to train with space capabilities that will be needed in combat.

The largest casualty of the above deficiencies appears to be the development of space-power thought. The lethargic attempts to stimulate this area are indicative of poor professional military education for space forces, deep-seated doctrinal beliefs and differing space force structures that allow varying degrees of integrated training and exercises. It appears that a more universal training curriculum would better serve the needs of the nation by ensuring better interoperability and standardization of space asset training.

Leadership

Leader development of the early British and U.S. air arms was lacking in several respects. The entrenched ideas about war held the senior ranking officers in both countries and both services hostage and made it difficult for them to envision the full potential of aviation. With a few, very notable exceptions, most of them saw no reason to train their aviators in any different a manner than the other specialties of their services. The tactical-effects nature of all existing weapons up to this point in time also made it difficult for them to imagine that training for this new weapon should be done in any different manner. Obviously this tactical type of training was necessary, but the need for closer examination for different types of training that might be needed was totally missed. As it turns out, a full examination of the operational and strategic methods of war was needed at all levels of leadership development training, especially the junior through mid-level officers, before the full impact of this new weapon would be realized. The lack of specialized schools that encouraged innovative thinking would not emerge until the establishment of the Air Corps Tactical School in 1923.

Currently, the U.S. military services take three different approaches to the education of their space cadres. The Air Force is, as it probably should be, very pilot-centric. It has justification in this by the fact that it takes a pilot, who is intimately familiar with aircraft tactical and operational employment, flight characteristics and possible effects to lead the Air Force into battle. Unlike the other services, there are not several weapon types to choose from. While the Army has the tank, the artillery, the infantry etc in relatively equal proportions, and the Navy has its aviators, surface combatants, submariners etc, the Air Force has only one predominant "branch" that fights…its pilots. In effect, all other AFSC's are relegated to the support role so the pilot can achieve some effect....drop a bomb, drop a leaflet, insert special forces, jam radar, fire an air-to-air missile, etc.

While this may be understandable given the nature of the service's modus operandi, it can be a double-edged sword. It is only natural to assume that space would also be viewed from the Air Force culture as being in a supporting role. In doing so, it is possible that the necessary vision to develop capabilities to fight in and from space would be lacking, since space would be relegated to second-class citizen status. The current curriculum at the Air Force's professional education institutions shows a lack of space studies, similar to that of the U.S. Army between the World Wars. By placing primarily pilots at the head of the its and the DoD's space agencies, it not only sends a signal to its space cadre, but also may be unintentionally delaying the nation's progress in space.

The Army, having relegated its space assets to a 1-star command (currently headed not by a space specialist, but by an Air Defense Artillery officer)[69] is not only showing what emphasis it places on space, but also has no exposure, save an elective or two, of its future leaders to space in its primary educational institution, the Command and General Staff College. Its leader development at the senior level is little better, having only 2 courses in space at the War College. Finally, the telling statement on the Army Space Career web page mentioned above reeks of pre-World War II U.S. Army mentality toward aviation.[70]

Although the current head of the Navy's Space Command is an aviator, the Navy is making an attempt to correct its lack of emphasis on space. It has recently created the education branch of its space command, which it linked with the Naval Post Graduate School, in an attempt to place additional leader-development opportunities within reach of those officers who desire to

---

[69] Army Space and Missile Defense Command, Internet, http://www.smdc.army.mil/, accessed 30 March 2002.
[70] U.S. Army FA-40 web site, Internet, http://www.smdc.army.mil/FA40/requisite.htm, accessed 30 March,

branch into space. Though this is a step in the right direction, the Navy's continued general lack of emphasis on professional military education and the War College's meager space course offerings bode poorly for its success.

Without a serious reconsideration of the PME systems of the services, it is doubtful that military leaders will develop an appreciation for space power or that they will be able to develop the concepts of operation needed to ensure its maximum potential.

Organization

Both countries suffered badly from inter-service rivalry when it came to organizing their air arms. This was mostly driven by their concepts of employment, but was also affected by the realities of their own traditional force structures, logistical considerations and hierarchic command structures.

In addition to pure organizational issues, these countries had to contend with several other factors that were related to organizational thought; divergence in service policies for air, a general neglect of the air arm and differing acceptance levels of the concept of unity of command all affected how they thought about, and organized air units. The fact that competence as a sailor first was viewed as the primary determiner of a person's worth before and during World War II, is remarkably similar to the current U.S. Army's directions to its space (FA-40) cadre.[71]

The different rank levels of the various services' space components are telling of the varying degrees of importance they place on space. The Air Force component is headed by a 4-star and its space force (AFSPC) embodies both space and missile career fields. The Army has a 1-star at the head of its space cadre (ARSPACE) and it is contained within the Space and Missile

---

2002.
[71] ibid.

Defense Command (SMDC), which is headed by a 3-star. Finally, although the Navy has created a separate command, directly under HQ US Navy, it is headed by a 1-star and thus like the Army, lacks the political clout of the Air Force command.

These organizational structures and command level differences reflect the service-specific thoughts about space. They are designed to augment the "enabling" roles for space as they pertain to the individual services' war-fighting concepts and they disregard the potential strategic effects achieved by those forces.

Materiel

In the early 20th century, the British attempted to achieve efficiency in the materiel development, as did the U.S. in later decades. Despite both governments' best attempts, the individual services retained their divergent ideas on design, procurement and acquisition that seriously hindered these efforts. Especially in England, during the very early ages of aviation, it did not help matters that the new air weapon was more heavily dependent on and sensitive to changes in technology than previous weapons had been. This created a need for a more dynamic, responsive industrial base and shorter drawing-board-to-production times.

The lack of a single procurement system for the aviation of both services often meant that orders were placed with industry that were of conflicting designs, unpredictable regularity and limited quantities, preventing any possible efficiency of scale from ever being achieved. In the case of the U.S., the additional problem of serious export control laws due to fear of sensitive technology transfers, had to be overcome. Often times, development and orders were driven by the services' competition for funds and prestige, rather than operational requirements. The lack of a single aviation spokesman and differing concepts of operation often meant conflicting testimony before Congress that both angered and confused them, further delaying action.

Today, the Air Force has been named the executive agent for space and a separate line has been added in the defense budget for space. This allows the Air Force to separate its normal requirements from space development and hence allows the Air Force to more objectively view the other services' needs, as well as permits it some discretionary funding for those particular capabilities that it feels it needs and are under-funded or unfunded. However, since it also gives the Air Force the dominant position in budgeting for and procuring space capabilities in general, it makes the other services uneasy, fearing lack of emphasis on their desired capabilities. To help alleviate some of this tension, DoD has final oversight on development priorities despite Air Force dominance on the issues.[72]

Nevertheless, the other services have "hedged their bets" in the past with the Navy stating that it has unique needs and in order to protect them, will expand its participation in space programs outside DoD. It intends to "leverage" outside capabilities to meet those perceived weaknesses in the system.[73] However, the latest Navy study concluded that the naming of the Air Force as executive agent may cause additional problems for this strategy.[74] The Army sees unfilled space capabilities as well and recognizes that it will need to fund some of its own efforts and embed space technologies in all its new acquisitions.[75]

Like the British developments during World War II and the U.S. experience between the wars, the U.S. may be caught in a situation of uncoordinated acquisition efforts for its space capabilities. Some way to streamline and coordinate procurement efforts would better enhance development and fielding of space assets to meet the nations security requirements.

---

[72] Interservice Static in Space.
[73] Navy Space Policy.
[74] Report of the Panel to Review Naval Space.
[75] Interservice Static in Space.

Soldiers

Throughout World War I the British faced a serious manning and professional development problem. Though mostly caused by recruiting competition with civilian as well as other government agencies, it also had competition within its services by not identifying aviation as a branch unto itself. The result was that in addition to a general man shortage, aviation faced resistance from other branches, especially in the tight manning environment that existed later in the war. The airmen that the services did manage to develop showed a lack of commitment to their aviation units due to the temporary nature of that tour. No attempt was made to professionally develop airmen by exposing them to the latest thoughts on employment of aviation. Training emphasis was on tactical skills and thus delayed the full realization of the new weapon's potential.

The U.S. faced a similar situation between the wars. Though manpower never actually became an issue, the neglect of the air cadre by both the services and the government resulted in serious shortages in even technically trained men and the facilities to do so. Resentment among airmen grew as they were usually drawn from line combat units and temporarily assigned under officers of the signal corps, a non-combat branch of which aviation was a part. Later, the lack of grooming of "pure airmen" continued to exacerbate the issue by delaying creation of a cadre that fully understood airpower.

Failure to include U.S. aviation in exercises also delayed the technical development of airmen by limiting their exposure to battlefield problems and cooperation with other branches. Although the U.S. was inducting men directly into their air arms by World War II, the professional military education of these men was still limited to that of the basic branches, and this mentality was revealed when, in 1940, the Army closed the only aviation school that existed.

Today, the services treat the space career fields very differently. The Air Force inducts directly into their space component as a primary career field. The Army has created a space functional area, meaning that a space specialist can remain in that field once a certain level of competence has been achieved in his primary branch.[76] The Navy treats it as a sub-specialty that sailors are expected to serve in for a tour and upon completion of that tour, return to their regular "rate".[77]

In summary, all services are generally lacking in their devotion of curriculum to space, at all levels of professional military education. As stated above, the Air Force does perhaps the best job, but it is still a very small part of the Air University's curriculum and is relegated to elective status in most cases.

In many ways, the divergent ideas about space cadre development today closely resemble that faced by both Britain and the U.S. regarding aviation in the first half of the last century. Regardless of the service perspectives on space, it is obvious that they all could do a better job of preparing their cadres to be better space advocates.

---

[76] U.S. Army FA-40 web site.
[77] U.S. Navy Space Command career web site.

CHAPTER 6

CONCLUSIONS AND RECOMMENDATIONS

It is the goal of this paper to answer the question of whether or not the current space structure is sufficiently utilizing resources for the nation to maintain the lead in space that it has enjoyed for nearly 40 years. Although the analysis provided here cannot hope to be all-encompassing, through the DTLOMS framework it provides substantial insight into some critical areas that are a measure of force development efforts. It has shown that some remarkable similarities exist between the current space situation and that of the air arms of Britain and the U.S. in the early 20th century. From the comparison, it is evident that the current structure of space forces is showing progress in some areas and still lacking in others.

Much like the Haldane committee for Britain's airpower and the Lassiter or Lampert committees for that of the U.S., the aforementioned space commission found the current structure less than optimum for the nation's needs. It completed the report in January 2000 and identified five major points that are summarized as follows:[78]

1. Current and rapidly expanding U.S. dependence on space and the resulting vulnerability demand that space be recognized as a top national security issue. Only with Presidential leadership can commercial, civil, defense and intelligence space sectors work to ensure U.S. dominance in space.

2. DoD and the Intelligence communities are not properly arranged to meet the challenges of the 21st Century. Disparate space activities should be merged, chains of command adjusted, lines of communication opened and policies modified to ensure funding is deserved and received.

3. The relationship between the SECDEF and Director of the CIA is crucial to ensure development and deployment of space capabilities necessary to support the President in war, crisis and peace.

4. Space will inevitably see conflict. It is imperative that the U.S. develops capabilities to deter and defend against hostile acts in and from space.

5. Investment in science and technology resources, including people, is essential if the U.S. is to maintain its lead in space.

Current stated U.S. National Security Space Policy addresses DoD's responsibilities in four major areas: Space Support, Force Enhancement, Space Control and Force Application.[79] The first area deals mainly with launch systems and launch site development and ground station security, but the other three areas deal more with direct military aspects and applications for future war-fighting capabilities. In addressing these latter areas, the policy discusses the development, operation and maintenance of systems, plans and architectures to meet the requirements of the military services; ensuring U.S. freedom of action in space through programs such as Anti-satellite (ASAT) capabilities, survivability functions and integrated warning, notification, verification and reaction capability; and preparing to acquire and deploy space weapons systems. Clearly the nation has tasked DoD to prepare to fight in and from space.

These are the conditions that make the current situation in space closely resembles that of the services and their air power components early in the 20th century. Although all services are making an effort to develop their space components, they are doing it through the lenses of their respective service-specific views on war and war-fighting concepts.

---

[78] Report of the Space Commission.
[79] Presidential Directive on National Space Policy, September 19, 1996, Internet, http://www.ostp.gov/NSTC/html/fs/fs-5.html, accessed 20 March, 2002.

Although the air and the space mediums are similar, they are not the same. Consequently, though the Air Force is by far the most advanced in its efforts to create a mature space force, it is still lacking.

In addition to faulty service development, the picture for DoD as a whole also reflects that of the early 1900's. Distrust and competition between services is rampant and the U.S. Army apprehension is illustrated by comments of the Director of Force Development and Integration Center at Army's Space and Missile Defense Command in 2001:

> "Although the NRO and Air force have the largest investments in space, the capabilities provided and the integration of those capabilities are equally important to all the services. Any actions or decisions that do not protect the joint nature of our space forces…would cause irrevocable harm to the services' warfighting capabilities. The increased responsibility and authority given to the Air Force….must be balanced by increased oversight from the commander in chief of US Space Command, the Joint Chiefs of Staff, and OSD. Without this oversight, there is potential that space could become focused on support to a single service, its style of warfighting, and to its priorities. This would be contrary to the best interests of the Army."[80]

In summary, the current DoD structure does not correspond to an optimum environment for the development of a Military Space Culture.[81]

In order to better prepare the U.S. military to deal with emerging space threats and capabilities, the U.S. should:

1. Maintain current structure and foster inter-service cooperation while keeping the Air Force as the executive agent. DoD must ensure fullest integration of force development; it can only do this by demanding acceptance of the current structure while allaying fears of other services by retaining its oversight of major space-related decisions.

---

[80] Col Glen C. Colins Jr, quoted by Ann Roosevelt in "Interservice Static in Space", Air Force Magazine, September, 2001, 58.
[81] Lt Col J. Kevin McLaughlin, Military Space Culture, prepared for the Commission to Assess United States National Security Space Management and Organization, 1999.

2. Be wary that the current structure does not optimize space capabilities and there is danger in viewing space through the prisms of individual service lenses. Duplication of effort both within and without the DoD is wasting time and resources. Current R&D efforts need to be coordinated NOW to ensure interoperability in future systems.

3. Realize that, once space assets become war-fighters, instead of war-enablers, the need for a competent, coherent space force that "gets it right" takes a quantum leap and the time might be right for creation of a Space Force.

4. Ensure that when that division occurs, it proceeds along the lines of the 1947 USAF split. This would allow the preponderance of space DTLOMS functions to migrate to the new service while letting the other services retain enough control over their space-specific requirements to ensure their needs were met. This would mirror current Army and Navy aviation, which allows them to look after their service interests before their airpower is used to affect the more strategic objectives, usually serviced by the USAF.

In summary, we are on the cusp of a major shift in war-fighting capability, as space begins to transition from an enabling medium to a full-blown battlespace. As this occurs, the United States needs to reorganize its forces to ensure that its space capabilities develop in line with its national objectives. Experience has shown that failure to do so at the appropriate time only delays required force development efforts that are necessary before a mature service can emerge to serve the nation.

BIBLIOGRAPHY

Air Force Association. "USAF Space Almanac 2001." Air Force Magazine (August 2001).

Air Force Association. ", "Air Force gets a space related Twist." Air Force Magazine (November 2001).

Bowyer, Chaz. History of the RAF. London: Bison Books Limited, 1977.

Cooling, Benjamin F. Editor. Case Studies in the Development of Close Air Support. Washington DC: Office of Air Force History, 1990.

Cooper, Malcolm. The Birth of Independent Airpower. London: Allen & Unwin, 1986.

DeBlois, Bruce M. Editor. Beyond the Paths of Heaven: The Emergence of Space Power Thought. Maxwell AFB, Alabama: Air University Press, 1999.

Davis, Richard G. Carl A. Spaatz and the Air War in Europe. Washington DC: Center for Air Force History, 1993.

Finney, Robert T. History of the Air Corps Tactical School 1920-1940. Washington DC: Center for Air Force History, 1992.

Holley, Irving Brinton Jr., Buying Aircraft: Materiel Procurement for the Army Air Forces Washington DC: Center of Military History, 1989.

Johnson, Herbert A. Wingless Eagle Raleigh: University of North Carolina Press, 2001).

Jones, Neville. The Beginnings of Strategic Air Power, A History of the British Bomber Force 1923-39. London: Frank Cass & Co. Ltd., 1987.

McLaughlin, J. Kevin, LtCol. Military Space Culture, prepared for the Commission to Assess United States National Security Space Management and Organization, 1999.

Meilinger, Phillip S. Editor. The Paths of Heaven: The Evolution of Airpower Theory. Maxwell AFB, Alabama: Air University Press, 1997.

Raleigh, Walter. The War in the Air, vol I. Oxford: The Clarendon Press, 1922.

Roosevelt, Ann. "Interservice Static in Space," Air Force Magazine (September 2001): 58-62.

Spaceflight Now Web site, , http://spaceflightnow.com/news/n0004/12afspacebudget

Turabian, Kate L. *A Manual for Writers of Term Papers, Theses, and Dissertations*. 6th ed. Chicago: University of Chicago Press, 1996.

U.S. Air Force. Air Force Doctrine Document 1: Air Force Basic Doctrine. Maxwell AFB, Alabama: Air University Press, 1997.

_____. Air Force Doctrine Document 2, Organization and Employment of Aerospace Power. Maxwell AFB, Alabama: Air University Press, 2000.

_____. Air Force Doctrine Document 2-1: Air Warfare. Maxwell AFB, Alabama: Air University Press, 2000.

_____. Air Force Doctrine Document 2-2: Space Operations. Maxwell AFB, Alabama: Air University Press, 1998.

_____. Air Force Doctrine Document 2-5: Information Operations, Maxwell AFB, Alabama: Air University Press, 1998.

_____. Air Force Doctrine Document 2-5.2: Intelligence, Surveillance and Reconnaissance Operations. Maxwell AFB, Alabama: Air University Press, 1999.

_____ SpaceCast 2025. Maxwell AFB, Alabama: Air University Press, 2000.

U.S. Army. U.S. Army Field Manuel 100-11. Washington, DC, Office of the Secretary

_____. How the Army Runs, A Senior Leader Reference Handbook 2001-2002, Pittsburgh, Government Printing Office, 2001

_____. FM 100-18, Space Support to Army Operations. Washington DC, Office of the Secretary, 1994.

_____. U.S. Army Space Reference Text, Washington DC, Office of the Secretary, 1993.

_____. FA-40 web site, http://www.smdc.army.mil/FA40/requisite.htm

_____. Army Space and Missile Defense Command web site, http://www.smdc.army.mil/

U.S. Government. Report of the Space Commission, 2001.

_____. Presidential Directive on National Space Policy, 1988.

U.S. Navy. SECNAVINST 5400.39B: Department of the Navy Space Policy. Washington, DC: Office of the Secretary, 1993.

_____ Report of the Panel to Review Naval Space, Assured Space Capabilities for Critical Mission Support, Washington DC, Center for Naval Analyses, 2002.

U.S. Navy Space Command web site, http://www.navspace.navy.mil/.

Wolk, Herman S. The Struggle for Air Force Independence 1943-1947. Washington DC: Air Force History and Museums Program, 1997.

www.ingramcontent.com/pod-product-compliance
Lightning Source LLC
Chambersburg PA
CBHW081259170426
43198CB00017B/2843